D0013313

DATE DUE

A Background Note about
IDA B. WELLS: A Woman of Courage

When the Civil War ended in 1865, Ida B. Wells was not yet three years old. Growing up in Mississippi, she witnessed that period of our nation's history called Reconstruction. During Reconstruction, the presence of U.S. government troops enabled southern blacks to vote and hold office. But when federal troops withdrew in 1877, racist Southerners decided once again to put blacks "in their place." They passed laws that segregated the races and made it nearly impossible for blacks to vote. As if these measures weren't enough, they used lynching to strike fear into the black population. It was a terrible time for many African Americans. But one woman was willing to fight back. As an outspoken reporter and civil rights leader, Ida B. Wells dedicated her life to shining the light of truth on injustice. This is her story.

IDA B. WELLS

*A Woman
of Courage*

RUTH A. ROUFF

 THE TOWNSEND LIBRARY

IDA B. WELLS
A Woman of Courage

TP **THE TOWNSEND LIBRARY**

For more titles in the Townsend Library,
visit our website: **www.townsendpress.com**

Illustrations © 2010 by Hal Taylor

All new material in this edition is
copyright © 2010 by Townsend Press.
Printed in the United States of America

0 9 8 7 6 5 4 3 2 1

Townsend Press, Inc.
439 Kelley Drive
West Berlin, NJ 08091
permissions@townsendpress.com

ISBN-13: 978-1-59194-218-4
ISBN-10: 1-59194-218-7

Library of Congress Control Number:
2009944086

CONTENTS

INTRODUCTION

Little Rock, Arkansas, January 1920

The black prisoners on Death Row had accepted their fate. As they awaited execution, they sang songs about forgiving their enemies and meeting their Maker. They did not realize that Ida Wells-Barnett, the famous black reporter, had snuck into the jail to interview them. Now she was growing impatient. After listening to their sad songs, she rose from her seat and walked close to the bars.

"I have listened to your story," she said. "You have talked and sung and prayed about dying. But why don't you pray to live—and ask God to be freed? If you have all the faith you say you have, you ought to believe that He will open your prison doors."

The men looked at each other in amazement. They knew Wells-Barnett was a reporter, but was she also a miracle worker? She didn't look like one. She was tiny, barely five feet tall. Her hair was gray. Her face was careworn. Still, when they looked into her eyes, they saw a will of iron. For the first time since their troubles began, the men felt hopeful.

Ida spent two weeks in Arkansas interviewing people connected with what would come to be called the Arkansas Race Riot. Once back in her hometown of Chicago, she set to work writing a pamphlet about the case. In it, she told the true story of how the white planters had cheated the black farmers out of wages for the cotton they picked. When the black farmers had formed a union to fight for justice, the white planters had fought back. They had sent two armed men to break up the union meeting. In the scuffle that followed, one white man was killed. Afterward, armed bands of whites roamed through black neighborhoods, killing scores of innocent people. As the whites rampaged, they set fire to the blacks' property and stole whatever they could. When it was all over, five whites and between one hundred and two hundred blacks had been killed.

In the days that followed, none of the rioting whites had been put on trial. Instead, twelve black farmers were tried. While in prison, they had been beaten and given electric shocks to get them to confess. They had all been "defended" by court-appointed local white attorneys. No jury had taken more than eight minutes to deliver guilty verdicts. They were all sentenced to death in the electric chair. It was a mockery of justice, and Ida would tell the world so.

"I truly believe," she concluded, "when these facts are laid before the world, it will so open the eyes of the country . . . that the whole country will say, 'Let those men go free!'"

The following winter, Ida was at home when she heard a knock on the door. When she opened it, a young man said, "Good evening, Mrs. Barnett. Do you know who I am?"

"I do not," Ida replied.

"I am one of the twelve men that you came down to Arkansas about last year."

When the rest of Ida's family came in to be introduced, the young man said, "Mrs. Barnett told us to quit talking about dying, that if we really had faith in the God we worshipped, we ought to pray for him to open our prison doors. After that," he said, "we never talked about dying any more, but did as she told us. Now every last one of us is out and enjoying his freedom."

Ida was pleased that the young man had come all this way to thank her. Over the years, she had fought long and hard to achieve equality for her people. It was an exhausting struggle. There had been victories and defeats along the way. But whatever the outcome of her efforts, she always knew that she had given her best.

Why was Ida so determined to go to any lengths to win justice for her people? Why did she refuse to give up hope, even when others had? The answer lies in the example her parents, Jim and Lizzie Wells, set for her years earlier in a little town in northern Mississippi called Holly Springs.

CHAPTER 1

"Ida, show us how well you can read," said Jim Wells.

"Yes, Papa."

Seven-year-old Ida was happy to obey her father. Quietly, she put down her dust rag, took the newspaper from her father's hand, and began reading the day's headline aloud.

"Governor Ames Visits Marshall County," she read in a clear voice. Then she read the rest of the article.

Her father's friends, Chester and Bill, smiled and nodded. However, they weren't at all surprised. Why shouldn't the oldest child of Jim and Lizzie Wells be smart as a whip? Jim was a skilled carpenter and a leader in the community of former slaves. He was what was then known as a "race man," a black man who would go out of his way to help others of his race. When his white employer, Spires Bolling, had told him how to vote in the recent elections, Jim had gone ahead and voted for the candidates he thought were best. At this time, the different political parties had differently shaped ballots, so it was easy to see how votes were cast. When Bolling saw how Jim had voted, he was not pleased.

The next day, when Jim came to work, he found that he had been locked out of the shop. Without a word to Bolling, Jim bought new tools and opened his own shop. The shop was a success. And it wasn't only Jim who had earned people's respect. Ida's mother, Lizzie, was known for miles around as a most wonderful cook and a strict but loving mother.

"You've got a smart daughter there, Jim," said Chester. "She'll go places. Maybe be a teacher." Bill nodded in agreement.

"Ida, would you like to be a teacher?" Ida's father asked her.

"Yes—well, maybe," Ida replied.

Although she hadn't told anyone yet, Ida thought that someday she might like to write for the newspaper she read. As it was now, when she wasn't doing chores, she often had her nose in a newspaper or book. It was something both parents encouraged. As a slave, Lizzie had been forbidden to learn to read. Jim

Wells had been a little luckier. His father was a white plantation owner who had no children by his white wife. Jim's mother, Peggy, was a slave woman. Realizing Jim's intelligence, his slave-owner father made sure his only child learned to read. When he was sixteen, he apprenticed Jim to a carpenter.

By the time the Civil War started, Jim had met and married Lizzie. Ida, born in 1862, was their first child. When she was six, they sent her to a school which had been founded by a white man, a former Union army captain by the name of Nelson Gill. For his efforts to aid newly freed slaves, Gill was hated by many of the local whites. Some of them had tried to kill him. His wife, Margaret, a teacher at the Freedman's school Ida attended, was determined to give the black children an education.

One day before school, several of Mrs. Gill's students came to her, saying that they had been called ugly names and been forced off the sidewalk by some white children. In these days, it was expected that black people would get off the sidewalk to allow white people to pass. If they didn't, they could be fined or even thrown in jail. However, Ida, like her father, was not one to take things lying down. She was one of the students who complained to Mrs. Gill.

"It's so unfair," one of the girls insisted. "We weren't bothering them."

"Yes," Ida echoed. "It's our sidewalk, too."

Mrs. Gill listened to the girls. Then she came up with a plan. She would place herself in the center of a column of black girls who would lock arms to form a solid wall across the sidewalk. Would it work? They would see.

After school, Ida and her classmates linked arms with Mrs. Gill and walked down the tree-lined street. As they walked, they chatted merrily, as if it was the most natural thing in the world to walk arm-in-arm this way. Three white girls were approaching. They looked horrified when they saw who was walking toward them. They knew they would either have to come into direct contact with the black girls and their teacher or get out of their way. They got out of their way.

After a few days of this, the taunting and teasing stopped. Through this example, young Ida learned there could be strength in numbers. It was a lesson she never forgot.

CHAPTER 2

"Yellow fever!"

"Oh my Lord!"

Ida heard her grandparents talking. It was the summer of 1878, and she was on vacation from Shaw University, visiting them at their farm in Tippah County, Mississippi. They had just learned that the yellow fever epidemic, which had started in New Orleans, had now reached Memphis, Tennessee.

Spread by mosquitoes, yellow fever was a dreadful way to die. The first symptoms were high fever, chills, a severe headache, and back pains. These were followed by vomiting and bleeding under the skin. Then the disease affected the liver, giving the skin a deathly yellow color. Finally came increased vomiting, kidney damage, delirium, coma, and death. There was no cure.

"Do you think the fever will reach Holly Springs?" asked Ida's grandmother. She sounded fearful.

"Don't worry," her grandfather told her. "If it does, Jim will take the family to Belle and William's." Belle was Lizzie's sister, and William was her husband. They lived in DeSoto County. It was a place the Wells family often visited.

Ida was still visiting her grandparents in late September. She had helped them harvest their crops, but had recently fallen ill with a mild case of malaria. As she lay in bed, she heard the sound of horses. Then she heard a knock at the door. Since everyone else was out in the fields, she got out of bed to see who it was. She recognized the three men standing there as neighbors from Holly Springs. Their sad looks told Ida that the news they brought was not good.

Without a word, one of the men handed her a letter. When she read it, the words leapt out at her. "Jim and Lizzie Wells have both died of the fever," it began. "They died within twenty-four hours of each other. The children are all at home, and a visiting nurse is taking care of them. Send word to Ida."

"Oh God!" cried Ida and sank to the floor.

When Ida's grandparents and aunt and

uncle returned from the fields, the house became a place of mourning. Ida wanted to go home at once, but her grandparents forbade it. However, when they got word that the epidemic had lessened, they gave in. Passenger trains had stopped running, so on October 10, Ida climbed aboard the caboose of a freight train and returned home.

Shortly after her return, there was a gathering of Masons at the Wells's home. The Masons were a club made up mostly of men in the building trades. Since Jim Wells had been a master Mason, the Masons felt responsible for his six children.

"My wife and I are willing to take in Annie," said one of the Masons, Bob Miller.

"And my wife and I are willing to take in the other little girl, Lily," said a man named James Hall.

Two other men were willing to apprentice Ida's younger brothers to learn their father's trade.

But no one wanted Ida's sister, Genie, whose curved spine made her unable to walk. She would be sent to the poorhouse. Ida was horrified. "It would make my father and mother turn over in their graves to see us scattered like that," she told the gathered men.

They looked surprised. "So you intend to keep the family together?" asked Bob Miller.

Ida nodded.

"How?"

"I'll get a job."

"Doing what?"

When Ida didn't immediately reply, James Hall suggested she get a job teaching in a school out in the countryside.

"You're sixteen. That's old enough. All you have to do is pass a written exam. You're smart, Ida. You can easily pass the test."

Ida agreed with the men on this point. She decided that she would follow their advice and seek a teaching job.

But first there was another problem Ida had to take care of. When her father was ill, Genie had seen a white visiting nurse going through his pockets. As a result, Genie had asked Dr. Gray, a white man whom she trusted, to safeguard the $300 that her father had saved and kept at home. That money would make a big difference in Ida's ability to keep the family together. She knew she must ask for it back.

A few days later, Ida walked to the town square to meet Dr. Gray. The square was crowded. It was commissary day—the day when groceries, clothing, shoes, and other necessities were sold or donated to surviving citizens. When Ida walked up to Dr. Gray, he smiled kindly down at her.

"So you are Genie's big sister," he said. He told her that he would bring the money around that evening. Then he went on to praise Ida's father.

"Your father would be passing through the court house, which was used as a hospital, on his way to the shop," he said. "If he passed a patient who was out of his head, he would stop to quiet him. If he were dying, he would kneel down and pray with him, then pick up his tools and go on with the rest of the day's work. Everyone liked him and missed him when he was gone."

Although these words brought tears to Ida's eyes, they also filled her with pride. She knew then that she would do her best to live up to her father's example.

True to his word, that evening Dr. Gray brought the $300 he had safeguarded to Ida at the Wells's house and then left for home. It was a perfectly innocent occasion. Yet, as Ida would soon learn, some people had overheard Ida asking Dr. Gray for money in the town square. In their minds, that could mean only one thing: that Ida had been asking Dr. Gray for money in return for sexual favors.

Now gossip was spreading throughout town about Ida and Dr. Gray. Although Ida was shocked by these rumors, they only added to her determination. Within a few weeks, she had taken the teacher's exam, passed with flying colors, left college, and found a teaching position in a school six miles away from Holly Springs.

CHAPTER 3

"Teacher, teacher!"

Ida felt a tug on her skirt and looked down.

"What, Missy?"

"I don't have a slate!"

"I gave you one last week, Missy. What happened to it?"

"I put it down somewhere, and now I can't find it," said six-year-old Missy.

"Has anyone seen Missy's slate?" Ida asked the class. No one said yes.

Ida could only shake her head. There were so many children in the little one-room schoolhouse in which she taught. Fifty students, in ages ranging from 6 to 14. Ida tried her best, but there weren't enough books and writing slates to go around. What few supplies they had were old and falling apart. It wasn't fair.

"I'm sorry, Missy," said Ida. "I'll try to get some more slates when I get back to Holly Springs. But for now you're just going to have to follow as best you can."

Missy glumly returned to the bench she shared with seven other girls and boys. Ida could see there were tears in her eyes as she watched the girl to her right copy her spelling words.

Ida turned to write more words on the cracked chalkboard. She had just written the word *birthday* on the board when something flew through the air, hit the chalkboard, and landed on the dirt floor. Looking down, Ida could see it was a wood chip.

Ida turned to face the class. "All right, who threw this?"

No one said anything.

"Do I have to keep the entire class after school today?"

Little Earl McMillen raised his hand.

"Yes, Earl?"

"Sorry, teacher. I meant to hit Billy Sanders, but I missed."

"Why on earth did you throw that at Billy?"

"He called me a no-good horny toad."

The class giggled.

"I'll see you both after school," Ida sighed, then went back to her lesson.

This was a typical day at the little country school in which Ida taught. She liked her students, but her schedule was exhausting. Every Sunday afternoon, she would set out from Holly Springs by mule cart, leaving her younger brothers and sisters to be cared for by their grandmother. The country roads were unpaved and bumpy. The constant jolts set Ida's nerves on edge. When she got to the small settlement, she would stay with one of the local families during the school week. These families were all very poor. Their cabins had dirt floors and no running water, and there was never very much to eat.

On weekends, Ida would return home to cook and clean for her brothers and sisters. Things got even harder when Genie died, and her grandmother had a stroke. Now a friend of Ida's mother cared for the children while Ida was teaching.

Ida clung to her love of reading to get through this troubled time. After eating dinner and preparing her lessons for the next day, she lit an oil lamp and read the works of her favorite authors: Charles Dickens, the Brontë sisters, and Louisa May Alcott. In these books, characters such as Jane Eyre, Jo March, and Oliver Twist struggled against what seemed like overwhelming obstacles. They were orphaned, misunderstood, and poor. Reading how they made their way in the world gave Ida courage.

After two years of teaching in the country, Ida received a letter at Holly Springs. It was an invitation from her widowed Aunt Fanny, asking whether Ida and her two younger sisters, Annie and Lily, would like to come to Memphis. By this time, Ida's brothers were already out of the house, working as apprentices. In the letter, Aunt Fanny suggested that Ida could get a teaching position in the Memphis schools. It would be a lot easier than teaching in the country.

Ida wrote back immediately, accepting her aunt's invitation. Now, she had the chance to recover from her grief in a large city. In her diary, she vowed to be like the characters she had read about. Like them, she planned to do great things that would live on after her death.

CHAPTER 4

Walking down Memphis's bustling Beale Street with Annie and Lily in tow, Ida was impressed by the activity around her. At the DeSoto Fish Dock, boats brought in the day's catch, making their way past the steamboats tied up in the river. These steamboats took on passengers of all types, as well as thousands of bales of cotton. The heavy bales of cotton were loaded and unloaded by teams of strong-armed men. Usually the men sang as they worked. The smell of fried catfish lingered in the air. It made Ida's mouth water. Up from the dock were several blocks lined with black-owned businesses—groceries, saloons, barber shops, clothing stores, doctors' offices, insurance agents, and pawnshops. A few blocks farther up loomed the twin towers of the new Beale Street Baptist Church, a city landmark.

After getting settled at Aunt Fanny's, Ida found a position teaching in nearby Shelby County. She could travel back and forth easily by train from her aunt's house. In the meantime, she began studying for the exam to obtain a higher-paying position in the Memphis city schools. She looked forward to using part of the salary she earned to attend the theater and concerts and meet people her own age.

Yet one day in May, 1884, something happened which cast a shadow over all the pleasant dreams Ida had about her future in Memphis. While riding back to her school one morning, she took a seat in the ladies' coach car as usual. There were no segregated cars then, since after the Civil War, Congress had declared segregation illegal. But the tide was turning once again. Southern racists were attempting to redraw the color line on the railroads. When the white conductor came back to take Ida's ticket, he frowned at her, then handed it back.

"I can't take this here," he said. "You'll have to go to the colored car."

"But that car's a smoker, and I paid for a first-class ticket in the ladies' car."

In these days, ladies often liked to sit apart from men, who often smoked, spat tobacco, and even got drunk on trains.

"I will treat you like a lady, but you must go

to the colored car," insisted the conductor.

"I refuse!"

Growing angry, the conductor tried to drag Ida out of her seat, but she would not give in. The moment the conductor caught hold of her arm, she fastened her teeth in the back of his hand. The conductor howled in pain, then went forward and got the baggage handler and another man to help drag Ida to the other car. The white passengers clapped and cheered their efforts.

By this time, the train had stopped at the first station. Rather than take a seat in the crowded smoking car, Ida got off the train. When she got back to Memphis, she hired a black lawyer to file a lawsuit against the railroad for her. When she found out he had been bought off by the railroad, she hired a sympathetic white lawyer, Judge Greer, to represent her.

In the meantime, Ida had begun teaching in the Memphis public schools and no longer had to ride the train each day. When her case finally came to trial, Judge James O. Pierce, a Union veteran from Minnesota, ruled that Ida had been discriminated against and awarded her $500. The railroad appealed the case. They were nervous and tried to tarnish Ida's reputation by hiring a black man to seduce her. This would prove that Ida was no "lady," and the railroad could blackmail her into dropping the suit. The plot failed. But the case would have to wait until 1887 to be decided.

Meanwhile, Ida had discovered new outlets for her talents. Eager to take part in Memphis's cultural life, she joined a club for black teachers. There she listened to concerts and took part in debates and dramatic readings. In one performance, Ida played Shakespeare's Lady Macbeth. "Out, out, damned spot," she cried, as she tried to wash the blood of murdered King Duncan from her hands.

The club also published a newspaper called the *Evening Star*. After contributing a few articles to the *Star*, Ida was chosen to be its editor. It was a job she accepted with enthusiasm. With more and more freed slaves learning to read, more and more black newspapers had become self-supporting. Ida knew the challenges that her audience experienced; she had gone through many of them herself.

"I wrote in a plain, commonsense way on the things which concerned our people," she later described her earliest newspaper columns. "I never used a word of two syllables where one would serve the purpose." She signed her columns "Iola." It was what her younger sisters and brothers had called her as a child.

From the beginning, "Iola" was sharply critical of black people who, in her opinion, weren't doing enough to help their community. One black "leader" whom Iola criticized was former U.S. senator Blanche K. Bruce, a former slave. Bruce had risen to political power immediately after the Civil War. At this time, the Republican Party, the party of Lincoln, held power in the South. In the early 1880s, however, Southern Democrats began to take back power. As a result, Bruce lost much of his political influence. Still, he owned three thousand acres of Mississippi farmland and belonged to a social circle made up mainly of whites. It bothered Ida when wealthy blacks like Bruce failed to speak out about the injustices that less fortunate blacks faced.

"Tell me," Ida demanded, "what good is a 'leader' if he does not devote his time, talent, and wealth to helping those less fortunate?"

It wasn't long before Ida's fiery words got the attention of other black newspaper editors. Some did not like her criticisms of well-known blacks, since they had social and political ties with them.

"Who does she think she is?" they asked. But even her enemies had to agree that Ida was a talented writer. Before long, she was contributing articles to *The Living Way*, a leading church publication. Soon after that, she began getting published in the *Washington Bee* and the *New York Globe*, two of the nation's leading black newspapers. It would be the *Globe's* outspoken editor, T. Thomas Fortune, who would, in a few years, help Ida in the midst of a crisis.

CHAPTER 5

In 1887, Ida's case against the railroad went to the Tennessee Supreme Court. Although Ida had hoped for the best, Chief Justice Peter J. Turney, a die-hard Confederate, led the other justices in ruling against her. In their view, Ida had no right to sit in the ladies' car, since there was a colored car available. They completely ignored the fact that the colored car provided seats for men of both races who smoked, chewed tobacco, and even drank. Therefore, it was hardly equal to the white car.

Ida was deeply disappointed. Unfortunately, the ruling was sadly typical of Southern efforts in these days to draw the color line. Throughout the South, whites were passing Jim Crow laws which strictly upheld racial segregation. In addition, white politicians were passing laws designed to make it very hard for blacks to vote. The adoption of poll taxes meant that voters had to pay a fee before voting. Other laws required that blacks, but not whites, prove they could read.

During this time, Ida thought that whites would naturally treat blacks better if more blacks became "respectable" citizens. Two incidents which occurred in 1889, however, caused Ida to change her point of view.

Three years earlier, Ida had read that Eliza Woods, a black cook in Jackson, Tennessee, had been accused of poisoning the white woman she worked for. Before she could stand trial, Woods had been taken from the county jail, stripped naked, and hanged in the public courthouse square. There, her body had been shot at and left exposed to view. Woods' lynching sickened Ida. But at the same time, she thought that perhaps Woods had been guilty. Now, she was horrified to learn that the poisoning victim's husband had finally broken down and confessed to the crime.

Another incident which aroused Ida's fury occurred in Montgomery, Alabama. There, a mob of angry whites had run a black editor, Jesse Duke, out of town. Duke's "crime" had been to question a rape charge that had gotten a black man lynched the year before. In his editorial, Duke had suggested that the relationship between the black man and the white woman was not rape, but a love affair. Southern white men were outraged by the idea that a white woman could fall in love with a black man. In their view, white women were pure beings who had no sexual desires. Black men, on the other hand, were lustful brutes. Therefore, any sexual relationship between white women and black men had to be the result of rape. This was how white men usually justified lynching, which was becoming more and more common throughout the South.

By this time, Ida had become editor of the black *Memphis Free Speech*. She used her newspaper column to call attention to the cases of Woods, Duke, and others like them. She was also still teaching full-time, but growing more and more discouraged about her job. The conditions in Memphis's black public schools were really not much better than black schools in the rest of the country. Furthermore, Ida had noticed that some of the newer black women teachers had benefited from their "friendships" with powerful white men to get teaching positions. In one article, Ida told the truth as she saw it. She accused school board members of neglecting black schools, and of giving young black women teaching positions in exchange for sexual favors.

One day Ida received a letter in the mail. It was from the Memphis Board of Education. When she read the letter, she learned that her teaching contract would not be renewed. She now had to earn her living from editing the *Free Speech*, whose circulation was low—only about 1,500 copies a week. It would be difficult, but she was determined to find new readers by making trips to outlying areas to sell subscriptions. Ironically, the same train system that had discriminated against her now proved helpful, for journalists were given passes to ride for free.

And so, Ida traveled throughout Tennessee and northern Mississippi, drumming up interest in her newspaper. It wasn't pleasant riding in the smoky "colored" cars, but Ida knew there wasn't any other way to win new readers. Her efforts were rewarded.

People who had heard of her were delighted to meet her in person. These people, in turn, introduced her to other audiences. In Water Valley, Mississippi, Ida was introduced by the grand master of the Masonic Lodge as the famous Iola. "I feel at home here," she told the gathering, "for I am the daughter of a Master Mason, Jim Wells."

Ida went on to talk about the importance of keeping the African American community informed. "It is only by standing united," she explained, "that we can battle back against the forces which are doing their best to keep us down." She came out of the meeting so weighted down with silver dollars that she had to go immediately to a bank to deposit them.

At the state bar association of black attorneys, Ida also received subscriptions from every man present. By March, 1892, the paper's circulation had risen from 1,500 to 4,000, a jump of over 250 percent.

But as hard as she worked during this time, life wasn't all work for Ida. As an attractive young woman, she now had several young male admirers. These young men called on her at home, escorted her to church, wrote her romantic letters, and generally hoped that she would return their affections. One was a schoolteacher, Mr. I. J. Graham. Graham was young, ambitious, hard-working, and thrifty. But Ida's beauty and keen intelligence made him bashful. After months of courtship, she grew tired of his shyness, and the relationship fizzled.

Another suitor was Mr. Louis M. Brown, a smooth-talking, self-confident newspaperman. Brown kept Ida off balance—declaring his love for her one minute, ignoring her the next. In the end, however, Ida realized that she did not love Brown, so this courtship ended as well.

When would Ida find someone to love? She didn't know. But she wasn't one to sit around feeling sorry for herself. Instead, she threw herself into her work.

CHAPTER 6

A familiar face appeared inside the entrance to Ida's office at the *Free Speech*. "Got a minute, Ida?" Thomas Moss asked.

Ida looked up from an article she was editing and smiled. "Of course, Tommie. Have a seat."

"Don't mind if I do," Tommie grinned as he put down his letter sack and sat down. Thomas Moss not only delivered the mail every day to the *Free Speech*; he and his wife, Betty, were also Ida's good friends. When their little girl, Maurine, was born, Ida had agreed to become her godmother. Also, Tommie and Ida taught Sunday school together at church.

"So, what's the news today?" Ida asked Tommie. Since the *Free Speech* was at the end of his postal route, when news happened in the black community, Ida usually heard it first from Tommie.

This time Tommie smiled slyly. "The news I have today," he announced, "is about myself."

"It must be very important, then," Ida joked.

Tommie chuckled. Then he went on to explain that he had saved enough money from his postal job to start a business. The previous afternoon, he and two business partners had signed the lease on a building in a suburb of Memphis called the Curve. This was where the city trolley tracks curved around. In a few months they would open a grocery store there. Since the Curve was home to a large number of black families, Tommie and his partners expected the grocery to do well.

"That's wonderful news, Tommie. I know you'll be successful." Then a shadow crossed Ida's face. "Isn't there a white grocery store out there?"

Tommie nodded. "Yes, there is. But William Barrett overcharges people and sells liquor under the counter. We aim to charge people fairly and run a clean place."

Still, Ida was concerned. "How do you think Barrett is going to take it when you open on his turf?"

Ida knew that most Southern whites didn't like competition from black-owned businesses. There had been reports from around the country that some had been burned to the ground. But not in Memphis . . . so far.

Tommy shrugged. "He probably won't like it. But what can he do?" When Ida frowned, Tommie added, "I've got a gun, Ida."

This put both of them in a sober mood. Then Tommie brightened. "Oh, well, let's not think of that now. But I do expect the *Free Speech* to cover our grand opening."

"You can count on that!" said Ida.

When Tommie left, Ida returned to her work. She was proud of Tommie and wished him the best. Still, a nagging fear tugged at her.

True to Ida's word, the *Free Speech* did cover the grand opening of the People's Grocery. It was a banner day for the black community. Tommie had hired a three-piece band and gave out free balloons to the children. After the ribbon-cutting ceremony, blacks began to flock to Tommie's grocery. It had better prices than Barrett's grocery and treated black customers with respect. Even a few white shoppers seemed to prefer the People's Grocery to Barrett's. Just about everyone was happy—except William Barrett.

Ida was visiting Natchez, Mississippi on newspaper business when a report came over the telegraph wire: Tommie Moss and his partners had been lynched!

CHAPTER 7

It had all started with a game of marbles between a black boy and a white boy. One did something the other didn't like. They got into a fight. When the black child, Armour Harris, began to get the better of the white boy, Cornelius Hurst, Hurst's father appeared and began to hit Armour. At that point, Will Stewart and Calvin McDowell came out of the People's Grocery to help the black boy defend himself. Soon, a mob had formed, with blacks and whites fighting each other. During the scuffle, William Barrett, the white owner of the competing grocery store, was clubbed. He identified Will Stewart as the man who had attacked him.

The next day, March 3, Barrett returned to the People's Grocery with a police officer. Calvin McDowell came to the door and told the men that no one matching Will Stewart's description was inside the store. At that point, Barrett became so angry that he struck McDowell with his revolver and knocked him down. When the gun dropped to the ground, McDowell picked it up and shot at Barrett, barely missing him. McDowell was later arrested but released Friday under bond. In the meantime, an arrest warrant was also issued for Will Stewart and Armour Harris. These arrests enraged the black Curve residents. They had never liked Barrett, whom they blamed for operating a "low dive" which sold liquor under the counter. Now they met to talk over the situation.

The white grocery-store owner pointed to this meeting as evidence that the blacks were plotting against whites. He got the ear of Julius Dubose, judge of the Shelby County criminal court. DuBose, a former Confederate soldier, vowed to protect the whites. He decided to form a posse to get rid of the "high-handed rowdies" in the Curve. To add to the tense situation, on Saturday, March 5, John Mosby, a black painter, was shot and killing by a clerk in another white grocery in the Curve area. Fearful that their property would be attacked, the People's Grocery owners met with a lawyer. The lawyer told them that since they were outside the city limits, they should prepare to defend themselves.

On the night of Saturday, March 5, six armed white men, including a county sheriff and plainclothes deputies, made their way to the People's Grocery. About ten o'clock that night, Moss was going over his accounts for the week. Calvin McDowell and his clerk were waiting on the last customers of the evening. A few minutes after the last customers left, shots rang out in the back of the store. McDowell and Stewart had seen several white men sneaking through the rear door. Thinking the men were about to attack, they fired on them. Three of these men were seriously wounded, one in the eye. The others gave the alarm. In the meantime, more deputized whites came on the scene. They arrested a total of thirteen blacks and seized weapons and ammunition that had been found inside the grocery.

In the aftermath, white newspapers reported the shootings as a cold-blooded ambush of whites. Accounts in black newspapers, however, painted a different picture. They pointed out that as soon as the black men realized the intruders were lawmen, they dropped their weapons and allowed themselves to be arrested. They were confident that they would be able to explain their case in court.

After the men were arrested, armed whites gathered around the Shelby County Jail. They muttered about what they would do with the black prisoners if one of the white deputies died.

On Monday, March 7, Betty Moss, Tommie's pregnant wife, went to the jail. "I've come to bring my husband some supper," she told Judge DuBose.

"I'm in no mood to grant visiting rights," he replied. "Come back in three days." But it was later believed by Ida and other black leaders that DuBose knew that Moss had only two days to live.

On Tuesday, March 8, it was learned that the injured deputies were not going to die after all. At first, black citizens of Memphis were relieved. But this news actually led to mob violence, since the black men could not now be legally executed for their "crime."

Late at night on March 9, 75 men wearing black masks surrounded the Shelby County Jail. They already knew which prisoners they wanted. When they found Moss, Stewart, and McDowell, they dragged them out of their cells and took them to a railroad yard about a mile outside of the city. There, they shot them to death. When the three bodies were found, the fingers of McDowell's right hand had been shot to pieces, and his eyes were gouged out. White reporters wrote up the murders in such gory detail that it was clear that they had been called in advance to witness the lynching. The newspapers quoted Moss's last words: "Tell my people to go west—there is no justice for them here." When the lynchers went through Tommie Moss's pockets, they found a publication from the Sunday school at which he taught.

When news reached the whites that shocked blacks were massing at the Curve, Judge DuBose ordered the sheriff to "take a hundred men, go out to the Curve at once, and shoot down on sight any Negro who appears to be making trouble." Armed mobs of whites obeyed the judge's orders. They shot into groups of blacks as if they were on a hunting trip. The mob also took possession of the People's Grocery Store and destroyed what they could not eat or steal. The creditors then closed the store. A few days later, what remained of the stock was sold at auction. The purchaser was William Barrett.

Tommie Moss had already been buried by the time Ida got off the train in Memphis, tired and heartsick. Making her way down Beale Street, she entered her office and sat at her desk. Looking around, she recalled all the pleasant times she had spent chatting with

Tommie. Although stunned by the lynching, she knew she must gather her strength to put out a new edition of the *Free Speech*. At first, she feared that finding the right words would fail her. But then the right words came. In an editorial entitled "The City of Memphis," she echoed Moss's last words and wrote:

> The city of Memphis has demonstrated that neither character nor standing helps the Negro if he dares to protect himself against the white man or become his rival. There is nothing we can do about the lynching now, as we are outnumbered and without arms. . . . There is therefore only one thing left that we can do; save our money and leave a town which will neither protect our lives and property, nor give us a fair trial in the courts, but takes us out and murders us in cold blood when accused by white persons.

Ida's editorial struck an immediate chord with the black residents of Memphis. No sooner had the latest edition come out than blacks began preparing to pull up stakes and leave Memphis for the newly opened Oklahoma Territory.

CHAPTER 8

About six weeks after the lynching, two men from the Memphis trolley system came to see Ida at the *Free Speech*. They had noticed a sharp slump in the number of black trolley riders. "We want you to use your influence to get blacks to ride the streetcars again," they told Ida.

Since there were no Jim Crow streetcars in Memphis at that time, Ida asked the men what they thought was the cause.

"We don't know," one of the men said. "It may be that blacks are afraid of electricity, since it has been less than a year since the trolleys were electrified."

"I can't believe that's the cause," Ida replied. "The streetcars have been using electric power for over six months, and you're just noticing a slump. How long since you have observed the change?"

"About six weeks."

When Ida pointed out that the lynching had taken place six weeks ago, the men protested that the streetcar company had nothing to do with the lynching. "It is owned by Northern businessmen," said one of the men.

"And run by Southern lynchers," Ida shot back. "We have learned that every white man of any standing in town knew of the plan and consented to the lynching of our boys. Did you know Tom Moss, the letter carrier?"

"Yes," the man replied.

"A finer, cleaner man than he never walked the streets of Memphis. Yet he was shot down like a dog, simply because he was a man who defended his property from attack. The colored people feel that every white man in Memphis who consented to his death is as guilty as those who fired the guns which took his life. That's why they want to get away from this town."

"Why don't the colored people find the guilty ones?" protested one of the men.

"As if we could. There is a strong belief among us that the criminal court judge himself was one of the lynchers. You know very well that we are powerless in the courts."

"Well, we hope you will do what you can for us. If you learn of any discourtesy on the part of our employees, let us know, and we will be glad to remedy it."

After the two men left, Wells wrote an article about the interview for the next issue of the *Free Speech*. In it, she told the black community to continue to stay off the streetcars.

In the meantime, blacks continued to leave Memphis. As a result, white businesses which depended on black customers became alarmed. They published stories warning of the hardships undergone by those who had already gone west. They told of starvation and hostile Indians, and urged the black people who were still in Memphis to stay among "friends." Still, blacks pulled up stakes and left. It was difficult in Oklahoma, but many felt they had no choice.

Ida had already decided to leave Memphis and relocate the *Free Speech* elsewhere. Long before the lynching, she had planned to travel to Philadelphia to attend the upcoming convention of the African Methodist Episcopal Church. After that, she would head to New York City to meet with T. Thomas Fortune, the brilliant editor of the *New York Age* (formerly the *Globe*). Perhaps a northeastern city would become the new home of the *Free Speech*. So in the third week of May, 1892, Ida finished writing her editorials for the week and headed north. Although she didn't know it when she boarded the train that morning, it would be nearly thirty years before she would once again set foot in Memphis.

CHAPTER 9

T. Thomas Fortune, the slim, well-dressed editor of the *New York Age*, looked at Ida through wire-rimmed glasses. He smiled as he ushered her to a seat in his office.

"Well, it's taken you a long time to get to New York, but now that you are here, I am afraid you will have to stay."

Ida was bewildered by this unexpected greeting and said so.

"Haven't you seen the morning paper?" Fortune asked, handing her a copy of the *New York Sun*.

Ida was struck speechless by what she read. In a news report from Memphis, she learned that a committee of leading citizens had gone to the *Free Speech* the night before. There they had destroyed the office and left a note saying that anyone trying to publish the paper again would be punished with death. Fortunately, Ida's business manager had received a tip and left town before the men could attack him. The article went on to say that the paper was owned by Ida B. Wells, a former schoolteacher, who was traveling in the North.

As Ida read on, she learned that the white citizens had objected to an editorial she had written. In this editorial, she had challenged the idea that the root cause of lynching was outrage over the rape of white women by black men. She knew this was not the reason Tommie Moss and his partners had been lynched. Furthermore, she suspected that it was not true of other lynchings, as well. In the editorial, she suggested that some white women weren't the lily-pure beings they were thought to be. In most cases the sexual relationships between white women and black men were love affairs. Why shouldn't they be? For years, white men had been having sexual relationships with black women. Was it really surprising that some white women were attracted to black men?

At first, Ida thought it was the white mob's gallant defense of white womanhood that had led them to destroy her paper. Later, however, she realized that they had wanted to do so ever since she had begun encouraging blacks to leave Memphis. Her most recent editorial had given them a handy excuse. As in most of the South, whites in Memphis counted on blacks to do much of the work they were unwilling to do. In addition, many white-owned businesses depended on black customers to turn a profit. Whites would be hurt in the pocketbook if blacks left Memphis.

Ida took a deep breath and looked at Fortune.

"I'm very sorry," he told her.

"I appreciate your concern," she replied. When he suggested that she become a contributing editor of the *Age*, she gladly accepted.

As it turned out, she had little choice. In the next few days, friends from Memphis sent her letters and telegrams. "They're watching the trains and your home," the notes warned. "If you return, they promise to kill you on sight."

One white newspaperman believed that a man had written Ida's article. In an article, he wrote, "The black wretch who had written that foul lie should be tied to a stake at the corner of Main and Madison Streets. Then a pair of tailor's shears should be used on him, and he should be burned at the stake."

As if this weren't frightening enough, Ida's friends also sent word that black men were organized to protect her should she return. Fearing there would be more bloodshed, she decided never to return to Memphis. Instead, she would use the position Fortune had offered her to speak the truth about lynching to the nation.

On June 25, 1892, T. Thomas Fortune printed 10,000 copies of the *New York Age*. This issue contained Ida's inside story of Negro lynchings. In it, she presented facts and figures. Through the *Chicago Tribune*, she had learned that 728 mob killings had been reported from 1882 through 1891. Of these, no one had been accused of rape in nearly two-thirds of the cases. Most lynchings, she pointed out, were committed against blacks who had competed against whites or were simply "too sassy." In one infamous lynching, she noted that a black man, Edward Coy, and a white woman had been carrying out an affair for more than a year. When news of the affair leaked out, a white mob insisted that the woman accuse her lover of rape. Then they pressured her to light the match to the bonfire that burned him to death. In his final moments, the lynching victim begged his former lover to remember that they had been "sweethearts" for a long time. She lit the match anyway.

The June 25 article was a bombshell. After it came out, two respected black women from New York organized a program to honor Wells for her efforts and to raise money to publish her findings. As word spread and interest increased, Lyric Hall in downtown Manhattan was chosen for the program. There, Ida would have a chance to use her public-speaking skills on a stage greater than she had ever stood on before.

CHAPTER 10

"Without further delay, I present to you our distinguished speaker, Miss Ida B. Wells."

A large crowd applauded as Ida walked across the stage to the podium at Lyric Hall. She was grateful for the show of support. On either side of her sat a row of distinguished black women from as far away as Boston and Philadelphia. From Boston came Josephine St. Pierre Ruffin, who had helped Southern freedmen migrate to Kansas at the end of Reconstruction. From Philadelphia came Mrs. Gertrude Mossell, another leading black reporter. Dr. Susan McKinney of Brooklyn, a leading black woman physician, was also on the platform. Displayed in electric lights behind Ida was her pen name, Iola.

Nonetheless, as Ida began to read her speech, a panic seized her. So much had happened in the past few months. The lynching of Tommie Moss and the others, the threats on her life, the loss of her business and home . . . all of these made her feel lonely and afraid. Yet she knew she must speak out for all those who had been denied justice. Even as she struggled to gain control of her emotions, tears began flowing down her cheeks. Still, she continued to read what she had written.

Although her tears embarrassed Ida, the audience thought no less of her. Afterward, one woman came up to her. "Your speech was just the thing to convince New Yorkers of the seriousness of the lynching situation," she told Ida.

The women who had organized the event gave Ida five hundred dollars and a gold brooch in the shape of a pen, her chosen profession. She would proudly wear the brooch for the rest of her life. The money was placed in the bank, awaiting the time when she would be able to start her own newspaper. But more than these donations came as a result of Ida's speech at the hall. The force of what she had to say convinced several important black women that they needed to start organizations to fight for black rights. Mrs. Ruffin organized the Women's Era Club in Boston. Then she helped black women in smaller cities to organize their own clubs.

Secondly, the Lyric Hall speech marked the beginning of Ida's career as a public speaker. Soon afterward, invitations to speak came to her from Philadelphia; Wilmington, Delaware; Chester, Pennsylvania; and Washington, D.C.

In Philadelphia, Ida was the guest of William Still, who had helped countless slaves as they escaped north to freedom. Visiting Philadelphia at the same time was a Quaker woman, Miss Catherine Impey, of Somerset, England. The Quakers were well known for having taken the lead in the movement to abolish slavery. When Miss Impey learned that Ida was in town, she was determined to attend her lecture. She was powerfully affected by it. Afterward, she called on Ida at Mr. Still's home.

"I can't tell you, my dear," she told Ida, "how ashamed I am that even some of my fellow Quakers seem indifferent to the problem of lynching."

Although Ida didn't know it at the time, when Miss Impey returned to England, she spoke with some of her reform-minded friends. Together, these friends agreed that it would be a good thing if Ida could spread her anti-lynching message in England. Soon Ida would receive an invitation asking her to do just that.

CHAPTER 11

"I am so glad you came to speak here," Frederick Douglass told Ida Wells.

"It's an honor, sir," said Ida. She meant it. She only hoped that she could make a speech that Douglass would respect.

In 1893, Frederick Douglass was the most famous black man in the world. Born a slave in Maryland in 1818, he had escaped to become a leader in the struggle to abolish slavery. After the Civil War, he became the most powerful spokesman for the rights of his people in America. He had also developed close ties with white suffragists like Susan B. Anthony and Elizabeth Cady Stanton. Like them, he believed that all women should have the right to vote. At this point, he was 75 years old, and more and more willing to turn over the struggle for equal rights to a new generation of leaders. It was he who had invited Ida to speak at Metropolitan Church in Washington, D.C. Now, as well-dressed women and men filled the church pews, the "grand old man" of the struggle for black rights introduced Ida Wells.

As she had done in her previous speeches, Ida laid out the facts about lynching. "Contrary to what white Southerners claim about black men and rape," she said, "lynching is nothing more than an excuse to get rid of Negroes who are acquiring wealth and property. In this way, they try to keep us terrorized."

Ida went on to quote facts and figures to support her argument. Then she gave a moving account of the lynching of her friend, Tommie Moss. By now, Ida did not need to read her speech word for word. She had become a polished speaker and could recite it from memory. Nor did she speak with tears streaming down her cheeks. She had learned to control her emotions.

As she ended her speech, the audience broke out into applause. Better yet, by the end of the evening, they had donated a large sum to the anti-lynching campaign.

The next morning, however, newspapers carried the news of one of the most awful lynchings and burnings the nation had ever witnessed. In Paris, Texas, a four-year-old white child named Myrtle Vance had been found strangled. Suspicion centered on a black man, Henry Smith, a mentally disturbed day laborer who had recently been arrested and beaten by Myrtle's father, the town's sheriff. It was assumed that Smith had killed Myrtle as an act of revenge. When he ran away, two thousand men set out in search of him. During the course of the search, they had come across Smith's stepson. When he refused to reveal Smith's whereabouts, they lynched him. Finally, Smith was caught near Hope, Arkansas. The news sent the citizens of Paris into a frenzy of excitement. Schools and stores were closed, while a crowd of some ten thousand people, some who had come from as far away as Dallas, gathered to await Smith's return.

Once Henry Smith got to Paris, he was placed on a mock throne and carried through town to the main square. There, he was placed on a scaffold and his clothes torn off. Then, for the next fifty minutes, Smith was tortured. Red-hot irons were placed against his skin. His eyes were burned out. As he moaned in pain, the crowd cheered. Finally, a red-hot poker was thrust down his throat. When it appeared he was dead, kerosene was poured over him, and he was set on fire. Later on, people scoured his ashes for unburned body parts to keep as souvenirs. Photographers took pictures of the scene and sold them as picture postcards. Smith's screams had been recorded by a recent invention, the gramophone, and were sold as well.

Although evidence indicated that Smith was guilty of murdering Myrtle Vance, Ida knew that his case should still have been tried in a court of law. Determined to get the facts, she sent a white Pinkerton detective to Paris to investigate. From him, she learned that the townspeople had known for some time that Smith was insane. In an article on the case, Ida wrote about a black minister who had previously tried to get Smith committed to an insane asylum. The minister had told the detective that Smith had been acting crazy days before the murder of Vance. When the minister tried to stop the lynching by suggesting that Smith be committed, he himself was threatened with lynching and run out of town.

The Smith lynching sent shockwaves throughout the United States. Southern reformers wrung their hands over it. Northerners believed it proved that the South had sunk into barbarism. Now Northern white audiences, too, were eager to hear Ida Wells speak out about lynching. On February 13,

1893, she spoke before a mainly white audience at Boston's Union Temple Baptist Church. She began her talk by addressing the issue of their silence on lynching.

"I cannot believe that the indifference regarding mob rule is other than the result of ignorance of the true situation," she said. "Do you ask the remedy? A public sentiment strong against lawlessness must be aroused. Every individual can contribute to this awakening. When a sentiment against lynch law as strong, deep and mighty as that roused by slavery prevails, I have no fear of the result."

The white parishioners responded enthusiastically to Ida's speech. Many vowed to become active in the anti-lynching movement. But meanwhile, the white Southern press had gotten wind of Ida's campaign. They were determined to do everything possible to destroy her reputation.

"Ida Wells is nothing but a wench and a harlot," declared the white-owned *Memphis Commercial*. It also accused her of raising money for her own personal use and wanting to marry a white husband.

Fortunately, Ida's friends and associates in the black press rallied around her. One black newspaper, the *Topeka Weekly Call*, sniffed that Ida was clearly superior to her critics. In Boston,

Josephine St. Pierre Ruffin defended Ida's purity of purpose and character. Nonetheless, Ida wanted more than just the support of her friends; she was determined to sue the *Commercial* for libel. To do so, she met with a friendly white lawyer, Albion Tourgée.

"I'd like to take your case," Tourgée told Ida, "but I'm very busy now with another civil rights case. However, I can recommend a highly skilled lawyer in Chicago who may agree to represent you. He's a Negro gentleman by the name of Ferdinand Barnett."

Ida did contact Barnett, who agreed to take her case. In the end, they decided that it was too risky, and she reluctantly dropped the lawsuit. Nonetheless, she was pleased that the handsome, successful Barnett had been willing to champion her. She admired him, and it appeared that he, a widower, admired her. However, any budding romance would have to wait. Later in February, Ida received an invitation from Catherine Impey to depart immediately for the British Isles.

CHAPTER 12

"Anchors aweigh!"

The mighty ocean liner sounded its horn, then cast off from the New York City pier.

Ida had never seen anything like the ship she set sail on in mid-April 1893. It was huge and beautiful. She and her traveling companion, Dr. Georgia Patton, looked forward to exploring the finely decorated rooms and enjoying the first-rate service. However, during the voyage across the Atlantic, both women became terribly seasick. For days, they stayed in their cabin. Finally, on the ninth day, the ship docked. As Dr. Patton continued on to Liberia, Ida followed Catherine Impey's directions to Somerset. Once in Somerset, the two women traveled north to the home of Isabella Mayo in Scotland. It was Mayo who had arranged speaking dates for Ida in the British Isles.

Ida's talks received much coverage in the British press, most of it favorable.

Before one lecture, however, a gentleman asked Ida why the British people should be concerned about lynching. "I don't know much about it," he said, "but isn't it an American problem?"

But by the time Ida finished her talk, he and everyone else were outraged by lynching. The young woman whom Southern newspapers had condemned as a "disreputable colored woman" now earned the praise of British newspapers as a "sweet-faced, intelligent, courageous girl."

"This one looks good," said Catherine Impey.

"Let me see it," Ida said.

Catherine Impey, Ida, and some other friends were gathered around a breakfast table in London. They had finished their biscuits and eggs. Now they were poring over the daily newspapers, searching for the most complete coverage of each of Ida's lectures. When they found a good story, they bought at least a hundred copies of that paper. They then mailed the copies to important people in the United States. The goal was to get the message out to the American public that the British strongly disapproved of lynching. The newspaper clippings had their effect. Americans were stung by British criticism. Papers such as the New York Times began writing more disapprovingly about lynchings. Even some Southern newspapers were beginning to speak out against lynch law.

Yet in spite of Ida's and her friends' efforts, reports of lynchings continued to arrive during the tour. After a lecture in Manchester, England, an audience member read aloud an account from San Antonio, Texas. A black woman had been shut up in a barrel into which nails were driven. She was rolled down a hill until she was dead. In Memphis, another lynching had taken place. Before it was to be carried out, the lynchers sent Ida a mocking telegram inviting her to attend.

Despite these constant horrors, Ida never lost faith that things would slowly change. As she strongly believed, the way to right wrongs was to shine the light of truth on them. She planned to do so next on a huge stage—the World's Fair in Chicago.

CHAPTER 13

"That's a wonderful idea," exclaimed Ferdinand Barnett.

"I was hoping you would say that," Ida replied.

The two had been discussing the upcoming World's Fair over dinner at Ferdinand's home in Chicago. It was something the whole country was looking forward to.

The fairgrounds would extend over 686 acres in Jackson Park. There, the nation's leading landscapers and architects had created a glittering "city within a city." There were beautiful man-made canals and lakes. Stunning white-columned buildings showcased America's engineering triumphs. Nearby was the Woman's Building, which housed fine art and craft exhibits by women from all over the world. Above it all, the newly invented Ferris wheel raised fairgoers 260 feet above the ground.

Exciting as these exhibits were, Ida and Ferdinand had both been angry when fair organizers had refused to include a building dedicated to black culture and history. To make matters worse, the lone African display at the fair presented African villagers in a sorry light. The only black-run country which had a pavilion at the fair was Haiti. Frederick Douglass was in charge of that.

To help set the record straight, Ida had decided to prepare a pamphlet which would be given out free to all fairgoers. The pamphlet would explain to them why the fair had largely ignored African American achievements. It would showcase the progress made by blacks in 25 years of freedom and would be printed in four different languages.

"Since the fair will attract people from all over the world, it will be the perfect place to get the message out about lynching," Ferdinand agreed.

"Will you contribute an essay?" Ida asked him.

"I'd be delighted," he replied. In addition to being a successful lawyer, Ferdinand had helped to found a black newspaper, the *Chicago Conservator.*

"Father, may we be excused?" asked Ferdinand's son Albert. He and his brother, Ferdinand, Jr., were bored by this adult talk.

After the two boys left the table, Ferdinand and Ida continued their conversation.

Each enjoyed the other's company. Unlike some men, Ferdinand was not put off by Ida's strong personality. She, in turn, respected his dedication to the black community. It didn't hurt, either, that he was tall and good-looking. In Ferdinand's calm, mature presence, Ida felt protected. It was a feeling she hadn't enjoyed since the death of her parents many years ago.

Ida had been in the Windy City only a short while, however, when another lynching took place. The pamphlet, and Ferdinand, would have to wait.

The lynching had happened in Bardwell, Kentucky. The victim was C.J. Miller, who had been accused of murdering two young white girls. At the urging of Albion Tourgée, the white-owned *Chicago Inter-Ocean* hired Ida to investigate. Making her way to Bardwell, Ida posed as the dead man's widow to gather information. Her findings were published on the front page of the *Inter-Ocean*. According to Ida, after Miller was killed, it was proven that he had not been in Bardwell at the time of the murders. Furthermore, a bloodhound used to track the killer had lain down, accusingly, in front of a cabin owned by a white farmer just across the river in Missouri. Finally, a boatman had identified a passenger embarking for Missouri near the time of the murder as being either a white man or a very light-skinned mulatto. Miller had been brown-skinned. But the facts didn't matter. Miller had been hanged from a telephone pole and his body burned.

The publicity generated by Ida's investigation of the Miller lynching helped to spark renewed interest in her pamphlet project. Later that August, the pamphlet was published and distributed at Douglass's Haitian pavilion at the fair.

In her essay, Ida provided a short history of lynching. She pointed out that in most lynchings, blacks had not even been accused of rape. To discredit the idea that black men were especially likely to rape white women, she spoke of the Civil War years. During the Civil War, when most white Southern males were away fighting, not one case was reported of a black man raping a white woman.

"In 'free' America," Ida wrote, "yet another man had not been given the opportunity to defend himself in court. . . . It is the honest belief of many who witnessed the scene that he had been barbarously and shockingly put to death by those who claim to believe in Christianity, law, and order."

In a note at the end of the pamphlet, Ida wrote that people who wanted more copies should write to her; she would personally fill their orders. This was one reason she had decided to remain in Chicago. Another was Ferdinand Barnett. In the past year, Ida had come to look forward to Ferdinand's friendly, supportive letters. Now that they had had a chance to spend some time together, their feelings for each other had grown.

Still, Ida was cautious about committing herself to marriage. Remembering that at a tender age, she had to care for her younger brother and sisters, she was uneasy about becoming tied down. Yet she had to admit that settling in Chicago and marrying Ferdinand made a lot of sense. She was now writing articles for both the *Chicago Conservator* and the *Chicago Inter-Ocean*. And from another standpoint, Chicago was a challenge to Ida. Unlike many eastern cities, it still had no black women's club. Ida knew that it would benefit from having one. Without hesitation, Ida set out to form such an organization. By September, 1893, the Ida B. Wells Club had three hundred members.

At this point, Ida was almost ready to settle in Chicago for good. But once again, she received word from her British friends, who were urging her to return to Great Britain. This tour would cover even more ground than the first. During it, Ida gave 120 lectures, attended a garden party given by the Lord Mayor of London, and sat in on a session of Parliament. As a correspondent for the *Chicago Inter-Ocean*, she sent back reports describing what it was like to live in a city where all citizens were equal before the law.

"Here," Ida wrote, "a 'colored' person can ride in any sort of vehicle in any part of the country without being insulted; stop at any hotel, or be served at any restaurant one wishes without being treated with contempt; wander into any art gallery, lecture room, concert hall, theater, or church and receive the most courteous treatment from officials and fellow sightseers."

Ida's British lecture tour had the desired effect. A few months after she returned home, members of the London Anti-Lynching Committee set sail for America. Needless to say, white Southerners were not pleased by all this attention. They called Ida's attacks on them slanderous. Their newspapers referred to her as a "Negro adventuress" and worse. Nonetheless, it was clear that they were feeling the heat. North Carolina's governor felt moved to criticize mob action. Meanwhile, the governor of Tennessee promptly called for a full investigation of a recent lynching. Even the Memphis newspapers started to speak out against mob violence.

Ida watched these developments with mixed feelings. She hoped for the best, but feared that the behavior of whites in Memphis was due more to a desire to "save face" with the British than to a sudden concern for justice.

To keep up the pressure, Ida began a nationwide anti-lynching campaign. It was exhausting to travel from town to town for weeks at a time, but every now and then something happened which gave her new strength. Recently, she had received a letter from a poor Mississippi farmer.

"You must be supported," the farmer wrote. "To note that you are a woman (I might say a girl) and I a great big man and you are doing what I ought to do and have not the courage to do it, I think that sometimes it's a pity that I am alive, but all this talk won't make you better off nor does it help you in your work. Enclosed find one dollar."

Such letters were all that Ida needed to keep going.

CHAPTER 14

In the spring of 1895, Ida traveled to Rochester, New York. This liberal Northern city had been the home of Frederick Douglass. During her speech at the First Baptist Church there, most members of the audience seemed to accept the truth of what Ida was saying. However, one young man with a Southern accent rudely interrupted her.

"Do you think that all Negroes who have been lynched in the South were innocent?" he asked.

"I never claimed that," Ida coolly replied. "I simply claim that they were innocent in the eyes of the law. No man is guilty until found so by trial."

When she told the audience that she herself would return to the South when she did not feel she would be murdered for doing so, the Southerner again interrupted.

"If Negroes are so badly treated in the South," he sneered, "why do they not come north or go west or to some more agreeable place?"

Ida was about to reply when a silver-haired white woman sprang to her feet. Her face showed so much emotion that at first Ida thought she might be about to join in the white man's attack on her. She was quickly relieved, however, by what the woman had to say.

"I'll tell you why blacks don't come North," the woman exclaimed. "Because they are treated no better in the North than they are in the South." She went on to tell of a young colored girl who was told by her teacher that if she tried to attend her integrated school's benefit dance, none of the whites would come.

"The outrage on the feelings of that colored girl was the result of the same spirit that inspires the lynchings of the South," she concluded.

Ida appreciated this woman's remarks. After the meeting, the woman introduced herself. She was none other than Susan B. Anthony, one of the leading American crusaders for women's rights, including suffrage—the right to vote. As it turned out, she had admired Ida from afar. Now, when she had a chance to hear Ida in person, she took it. After the meeting,

Anthony invited Ida to stay with her and her sister, Mary, for the remainder of her stay in Rochester. They would have much to talk about.

Anthony, now 75, had been to England years earlier. She knew many of the same reformers whom Ida had met there. She was also a longtime friend of Frederick Douglass, who supported women's suffrage. But by now, many blacks had grown suspicious of white suffrage leaders. They felt that they had been too willing to go along with Southern racists in order to get them to support giving women the vote. As Anthony had guiltily told Ida, it had been she who had discouraged Frederick Douglass from attending a suffrage convention held in Atlanta that January. She said she had not wanted to see Douglass humiliated by racists. Nor did she want his presence to get in the way of bringing Southern white women into the suffrage movement.

"Was I wrong to do so?" Anthony asked Ida.

Ida could only reply, "Yes." However, she also knew that Anthony continued to have close ties with black reformers. The fiery women's rights leader had also spoken out publicly and privately against racism. Moreover, Ida would soon see for herself that Anthony was no racist.

One morning, before she went out on some errands, Anthony told Ida that she could use her private secretary to help her with her correspondence. At that time, people who had many letters to write often hired secretaries to take dictation in shorthand. It was a quick form of writing that made letter-writing faster and easier.

When Ida went upstairs to her room, she waited for the secretary to come in. When she didn't, Ida went on writing her letters in longhand. Later, when Anthony returned home, she found Ida busily at work.

"You didn't care to use my secretary, I suppose. I told her to come to your room when you came downstairs. Didn't she come?"

"No, she didn't," Ida replied.

Anthony said nothing, but turned and went into her office. Within a few minutes, she was back in Ida's room.

"Well, she's gone," Anthony announced.

"Who?"

"The secretary. I went into the office and asked her why she hadn't come to help you with your correspondence. The girl said, "It is all right for you, Miss Anthony, to treat Negroes as equals, but I refuse to take dictation from a colored woman."

"Indeed!" Miss Anthony said. Then she

added, "You needn't take any more dictation from me. Miss Wells is my guest, and any insult to her is an insult to me. So, if that is the way you feel about it, you needn't stay any longer." When the girl sat there without moving, Anthony told her to get her bonnet and go, and the girl got up and went.

Ida's stay at Susan B. Anthony's home ended pleasantly. Still, they disagreed on one important thing. Anthony believed that women were more "high-minded" than men, and that if they got the vote, they would naturally grant equal rights to blacks. Ida did not believe this. She had seen more than her share of petty bickering among women. Also, she knew that white women could be just as racist as white men. Despite their differing views, both leaders took pride in their relationship with each other. Years later, Susan B. Anthony published her autobiography. In it, she recorded her meeting with Ida. Later, she gave her an autographed copy. Ida, in turn, devoted a chapter of her autobiography to her meeting with Anthony.

Ida continued her speaking tour. That November, she concluded the tour with a meeting in Providence, Rhode Island, where Frederick Douglass was also scheduled to speak. It would be the last time she met with him—he died at his home in Washington, D.C. in February, 1895.

Ida was saddened by this news. Feeling exhausted, she knew it was time to get off the road and go home. Ferdinand Barnett had proposed to her, and she had accepted. Now a new life awaited her in Chicago.

CHAPTER 15

On the evening of June 27, 1895, nine hundred people filled the pews of Chicago's AME Bethel Church to witness the marriage of Ida Bell Wells and Ferdinand Lee Barnett. To the strains of "The Wedding March," a flower girl scattered petals to the right and left of the aisle. The bridesmaids were Ida's sisters, Lily and Annie. They had come from their home in California to attend. Both were dressed in beautiful lemon crepe, white ribbons, slippers, and white gloves. The groomsmen were handsomely dressed members of the *Conservator* staff. The best man was the newspaper's editor, R.P. Bird. Ida carried a bouquet of roses and wore a white satin dress trimmed with chiffon and orange blossoms.

Yet despite this happy occasion, Ida was already worried. Would she be able to balance marriage and career? In those days, it was unusual for women to have both. The reaction to Ida's engagement had not been positive. Some people publicly complained that she had deserted the anti-lynching campaign for marriage. As if to signal to them that she hadn't, her honeymoon lasted only one weekend. Early on Monday morning, she returned to the *Conservator* office. Now that Ferdinand was devoting most of his energy to his law practice, Ida would help run the newspaper.

Adding to Ida's sense of self-doubt, Ferdinand's mother, Martha, would be living with the newlyweds. It bothered Ida that Martha sometimes compared her unfavorably to her son's deceased first wife. In the years to come, there would be a number of clashes between these two strong-willed women. How Ida would manage to combine marriage with a career was a topic of gossip among some women. Many doubted that she would be successful at both.

Yet Ida had her own statement to make about the nature of her partnership with Ferdinand Barnett. She would not change her name to Ida Barnett. Rather, from now on she would go by the name Ida B. Wells-Barnett.

Whatever they felt about Ida's marriage,

African American clubwomen had begun to realize that their best hope of combating racism was to stand united. When a letter from a well-known white journalist appeared, condemning all black women as prostitutes and thieves, Boston's Josephine St. Pierre Ruffin knew what to do. Cleverly, she used the letter to convince other women club members to meet in Boston to form a national organization of black women's clubs. "The time has come to defend ourselves," she told them.

Although Ida was now pregnant and couldn't attend, she kept up with what was happening in Boston as best she could. She was proud when she learned the women had created the National Federation of Afro-American Women (NFAAW). By the time the NFAAW met again, in July, 1896, in Washington, D.C., Ida was prepared to attend. However, this time she would have her three-month-old son Charles and a nurse in tow.

The women now had an added reason to unite. That May, the U.S. Supreme Court had handed down its decision in Plessy v. Ferguson. The decision upheld "separate but equal" facilities. This was discouraging news to Ida. Like most Southern blacks, she knew from experience that separate facilities were almost always unequal.

At the convention, Ida gave a speech entitled "Reform." She was also pleased when the members praised her anti-lynching work. However, she disagreed with the decision to change the organization's name to the National Association of Colored Women. She liked the term "Afro American" better than the word "colored." The convention ended on a high note, however. When one member made a motion to name baby Charles the "baby" of the federation, everyone agreed. At this point, 75-year-old Harriet Tubman lifted baby Charles Barnett over her head before the audience. In this way, the past and the future met.

CHAPTER 16

Back in Chicago, Ida had a new goal. As a former teacher, she had always valued education. The first kindergartens had opened in America in the 1860s. Ida knew that kindergartens could benefit black children. Unfortunately, in Chicago there were few kindergartens that were open to blacks. To remedy this situation, Ida contacted Bethel Church's new minister, Riverdy Ransom. He agreed to help Ida establish a kindergarten within the church. Surprisingly, some black families objected to this idea. They feared that having an all-black kindergarten would lower the chances of getting their children into a white-run kindergarten.

"Are you so afraid of the color line that you will do nothing to help your own people?" Ida asked these critics. Ida and Ransom finally won out. A short while later, the first black kindergarten opened in Chicago.

Later in 1897, Ida gave birth to her second child, Herman. Even though the Barnetts had servants, Ida still had her hands full in supervising them as well as four children. Feeling overwhelmed with the burdens of motherhood, she announced that she was dropping out of public life. She told others that she looked forward to becoming a stay-at-home mother.

Ida's "retirement" lasted for only three months. In February, 1898, another horrible lynching awakened her spirit of protest.

Frazier Baker was the first African American postmaster in the small town of Lake City, South Carolina. White residents were not happy about his appointment. They claimed that his presence made the post office "not a respectable place for white gentlemen, much less ladies."

When whites set the post office ablaze and burned it to the ground, Frazier moved it to his home. There he set up a partition that divided his living room from the office. This move angered the whites even more. Things came to a head on the night of February 21. A large mob surrounded the Baker house and ordered

Frazier to come out. When he did not appear, the mob set fire to his house, forcing the family to flee outside. Once they emerged, the mob shot at them. Frazier was shot to death at once, as was his infant daughter, who had been cradled in her mother's arms. Frazier's wife and other children were badly injured. The following day, the badly burnt remains of Frazier Baker and his baby daughter were found outside what was left of the house.

Two days after the killing, Bethel Church was the scene of a mass meeting. This time, Ferdinand Barnett was one of the lead speakers. Since Frazier Baker had been an appointee of the federal government, Barnett and others challenged the administration in Washington to do something about the lynching. Ida spoke as well. "Of course Frazier Baker was a bad man," she sneered. "He held a public office when they told him not to."

Soon after, a collection was taken at Bethel for Ida to join Illinois state officials to travel to Washington to lobby the government.

Once again Ida was traveling, this time with baby Herman in tow. Charles was now old enough to stay with Grandmother Barnett. Although Ida felt somewhat guilty about leaving him, she felt that her efforts were needed to create a better world for him to grow up in.

In Washington, Ida was part of the Illinois delegation who called on President William McKinley. Members of the group urged McKinley to catch and punish Baker's lynchers and provide financial support for his family. Ida also told the president that national anti-lynching laws were needed. Her presentation was clear and able, and the Republican president was impressed.

"I assure you I will do everything I can to see that justice is done," President McKinley told Ida and the others. In the weeks to come, a number of the leading citizens of Lake City, South Carolina were indicted for the crime. But in the end, all were acquitted. McKinley lacked the will to challenge Southern racists on their home turf. Besides, he had something else on his mind: war with Spain

CHAPTER 17

In February, 1898, the United States battleship Maine exploded in Havana's harbor.

Two hundred fifty Americans on board were killed. Although it was unclear what had caused the explosion, many blamed Spain, which was fighting rebels for control of Cuba.

"Remember the Maine!" became a battle cry. In April, the United States declared war on Spain. Amidst all this commotion, Ida decided that it was a waste of time for her to stay in Washington. She returned to Chicago, where she helped organize a benefit for the Eighth Illinois Infantry, an all-black regiment.

From Chicago, Ida once again traveled to Rochester, New York for a memorial to Frederick Douglass. Once again she stayed at the home of her friend, Susan B. Anthony. However, when she had been at the home for several days, she couldn't help noticing the way Anthony bit out her married name when addressing her. Finally, Ida decided to comment on this.

"Miss Anthony, don't you believe in women getting married?" she asked.

"Yes, I do," Anthony replied. "But not women like you, who have a special call for special work." She went on, "I know of no one in this country better fitted to do the work you do than yourself. But now you have a divided duty. While you are here, you are distracted by the thought that maybe your sons are not being looked after properly at home. That makes for a divided duty."

Ida took Anthony's words to heart. She did often worry about her sons at home. But she also knew it was her mission to help her people.

During the memorial in Rochester, Ida and other black leaders formed the Afro-American Council. Ida was made secretary. The Council soon had its hands full, as a bloody race riot broke out in Wilmington, North Carolina.

What especially shocked black leaders about this riot was that in Wilmington, blacks had developed a prosperous middle class. A number of blacks had even shared power with progressive whites. Yet in 1898, racist Democrats staged a campaign to regain power.

They did so by playing on white fears of black men. A downturn in the price of cotton meant that white women were forced to seek work in the state's cotton mills. There they would come in contact with blacks. Aided by such secret societies as the Ku Klux Klan and Red Shirts, the Democrats laid out a plan to overthrow the city government.

On November 10, a mob of five hundred armed whites marched through town and overthrew the mayor, the board of aldermen, and the entire police force. Chaos followed, as the mob began attacking blacks. By the time the state militia was called in to restore order, 1400 blacks had left Wilmington, many under armed escort. Their abandoned properties were taken over by whites.

Ida was determined to force the Council to take action. When it was her turn to address the gathering, she criticized McKinley for his silence on the subject of Wilmington. "He is too busy decorating Confederate graves to speak out for us," she told the audience.

After the conference ended, Ida and other council members traveled throughout the Northeast, organizing local councils. They weren't on the road long when another horrible lynching occurred. This time, a black man, Sam Hose, had been accused of killing a well-to-do white farmer and raping his wife. On April 23, Hose was captured near his mother's house in Marshallville, Georgia. Special trains were provided for those who wanted to view the lynching. Once again, the victim's body was mutilated before being set afire. Once again, thousands of the area's "leading citizens" watched. Once again, fragments of the body were sold as souvenirs.

Shortly afterward, Ida spoke at Bethel Church to raise money to hire a white detective to investigate the lynching. Louis Le Vin, the detective, traveled to Georgia. To gather the facts of the case, he posed as a seller of medicine for hogs. What he learned was that Hose had argued with his employer, Alfred Cranford, for several days. Hose had wanted an advance on wages so that he could visit his sick mother. When Cranford drew a gun on him, Hose threw his ax at Cranford, killing him.

There had been no rape, since at the time, Mrs. Cranford had been seriously ill and was recovering at the home of her father-in-law. When Le Vin questioned some whites about the brutality of their treatment of Hose, they shrugged. Reporting back to the committee, Le Vin concluded, "I made my way home thoroughly convinced that a Negro's life is a very cheap thing in Georgia."

It was horrors such as these that caused some black leaders to despair. T. Thomas Fortune, for example, began to drink too much. But Ida pressed onward. In her pamphlet, "Lynch Law in Georgia," she wrote that her goal was "to give the public the facts, in the belief that there is still a sense of justice in the American people."

Ida hadn't lost faith in America. Would America reward her faith?

CHAPTER 18

Two middle-aged black women were strolling along together. Both were well-dressed and dignified.

"Ida says she's going to hold the charity ball where?" one asked.

"At the Pekin Theater."

"Isn't that the place Bob Motts runs?"

"Yes, I think it is."

"What in heaven's name is she thinking!" the woman sniffed. "Why, Motts used to run a saloon!"

The other woman shrugged. "Ida says he's turned over a new leaf," she replied.

The two women were talking about Ida's plans to hold the 1906 Douglass Center's benefit at the New Pekin Theater. The Douglass Center was an interracial group whose goal was to improve race relations in Chicago. Ida had been chosen to organize the benefit. The women were right: Bob Motts had operated a saloon. But Ida believed that people could change for the better. Certainly Motts seemed to have turned over a new leaf. He had hired more than a hundred black workers to turn his saloon into a top-of-the-line theater in the heart of a black neighborhood. There, patrons could enjoy skits, serious drama, music, and variety acts.

When members of the Douglass Center voiced their objections, Ida listened but did not change her mind. "I know all about Bob Motts's past," she told them. "But his new theater is a gem, and the acts he books are quite respectable. Since he has invested his own money in something uplifting to our race, I think we all ought to support him."

"Well, I think it will be a great advertisement for him," one woman sniffed.

An important black minister, Reverend E.J. Fisher, also refused to support the benefit. "You won't catch me going there," he preached. "If I ever do go there, may my tongue cleave to the roof of my mouth, and my right hand become feeble."

Another woman suggested that fine young Negro ladies would lose their reputations if they ventured into such a disreputable place as the Pekin Theater.

"They must not be very sure of their reputations if one evening at the Pekin Theater will ruin them," Ida cleverly replied.

Nonetheless, some members of the black "upper crust" threatened to boycott the charity ball. But as often happens, the controversy only added to interest in the event. Before long, tickets were selling fast. The event was a great success, and Ida was quite pleased. In years to come, the Pekin would feature a number of top-notch black performers, including musicians Scott Joplin, Jelly Roll Morton, Joe Jordan, and tap dancer Bill "Bojangles" Robinson. It also encouraged blacks to start theaters in other cities.

But Ida had little time to bask in the success of the benefit. In August, 1908, a white woman named Nellie Hallan accused a black man, George Richardson, of rape in nearby Springfield, Illinois. This time, police spirited Richardson away before he could be lynched. But the enraged mob unleashed their anger on the black population of Springfield. Before they were finished, they had lynched three other completely innocent black men and destroyed black homes and businesses.

The Illinois National Guard had to restore order. Two weeks later, Nellie Hallan signed a statement that said that neither Richardson nor any other black man had attacked her. The guilty party was a white man whose identity she would not reveal.

At this time, Ida was teaching a Sunday school class. It was clear, however, that her students' minds were on the recent lynchings in Springfield.

"What can we do about the situation?" asked one earnest young man.

"You've taken the first step by asking that question," Ida replied. Then she invited the students to her house later that day. Out of a class of thirty, only three showed up. But Ida encouraged these three to invite at least one other person next time they met. Soon, a spirited group of young people was meeting at the Barnetts' to discuss questions of race and black history. To give these middle-class young people some background in the problems faced by less fortunate blacks, Ida told them about the black emigrants who made their way to State Street, the Broadway of Chicago's black community. There the friendless men found only saloons, poolrooms, and gambling houses. Many of them had gotten into trouble in these places.

"We all need to do what we can to provide a safe place for these people," Ida told the young people who gathered at her house. They agreed. But where would they find the money to set it up?

One day, Ida delivered a speech at Chicago's Congregational Union. Several of the white speakers talked about the high rate of black crime and what should be done about it. When it was Ida's turn to speak, she did not challenge the statistics on black crime. Instead she pointed out that few, if any, social centers were open to blacks.

"The occasional black man who wanders into these places is very quickly made to feel that he is not welcome," Ida told the gathering. "Only one social center welcomes the Negro, and that is the saloon. Ought we to wonder at rising rates of crime?"

After the meeting, a white woman walked up to Ida, a look of concern on her face. "Am I to understand," she said, "that the YMCA does not admit black men?"

When Ida assured her that this was the case, the woman announced that she would tell her husband, who had donated a large sum of money to the Y.

A few months later, the same woman

called Ida and told her that her husband had confronted the head of the YMCA in Chicago. "I will never give you another dollar until you do something for colored men," he had said.

The woman's husband was Victor F. Lawson, owner and publisher of the *Daily News*. Now his wife was asking Ida what ought to be done. Ida proposed that the Lawsons help fund a modern, up-to-date reading room on State Street. In charge would be a hard-working young man. His job would be to visit saloons and poolrooms, distribute cards, and invite young men to the reading room.

"I'm interested in helping you," Mrs. Lawson said. Together she and Ida went to State Street to scout out a location. After they found a suitable place, Mrs. Lawson returned home to discuss the matter with her husband. When she saw Ida again, she told her that she and her husband were willing to help establish such a place and pay the rent for a year. And so, on the first day of May, 1910, the Negro Fellowship League Reading Room and Social Center opened at 2830 State Street. It was a bright, clean place which featured neat furniture and cases filled with books, newspapers, and magazines.

From the beginning, the Center attracted a large number of men. One Sunday it was warm, and the back door was left open. Ida and the others could hear loud noises coming from a group of apparently drunken men in the next yard. When the janitor volunteered to get the police, Ida hastily told him not to. She wanted to win the trust of the community and knew that calling the police wasn't the way to do it.

Going into the back yard herself, Ida looked through the fence into the other yard. There she could see about a dozen dirty, disreputable-looking men seated on the ground shooting craps. When she walked over to them and politely asked them to make less noise because they were disturbing the meeting, they looked amazed. Instantly every one of them got up except one, who was too drunk to do so. When they assured Ida they would make less noise, she invited them into the meeting.

"Oh, no, lady, we are too dirty. We would not think of coming in like this. But we will come back some other time."

And some of them did. The Fellowship Center stayed on State Street for ten years and was never again disturbed. Soon after this encounter, the Center added a men's lodging house upstairs. There, men could get a bed for 15 cents and a more private, partitioned sleeping space for a quarter. At the end of the first year, forty to fifty people a day were coming in to read, play checkers, or hunt for jobs. In time, employers began stopping by to find workers.

After a speech Ida gave to the men's Bible class in Oak Park, a white man came up to Ida with tears in his eyes. He, too, was amazed that the YMCA refused to admit black men.

"What can I do to help?" he asked Ida. He was Judge Jesse A. Baldwin, at that time chief justice of the criminal court. When Ida explained what was needed, Judge Baldwin became a lifelong friend of the Barnetts. Sometimes, he sent troubled young men, who had appeared in his courtroom, to them for help. Later on, Ida would become officially employed as an adult probation officer. The money she earned at this job would help to pay the expenses of the Fellowship Center.

CHAPTER 19

As much as Ida appreciated the help of friendly whites, the ugly truth was that most white Americans at this time were prejudiced against blacks. This racism was brought home to Ida once more when a lynching occurred downstate in Cairo, Illinois.

When the gagged corpse of Anna Pelley, a 26-year-old shopgirl, was discovered, Ida noted that the police followed the usual custom and "immediately looked for a Negro." Soon they arrested a coal driver named William "Frog" James. It was claimed that James owned a handkerchief similar to that found in the victim's mouth. There was no other "evidence" to connect him with the crime. When a lynch mob assembled, the Illinois National Guard was called in. James was taken 25 miles away to a small town. But the mob tracked him down, took him from his jail cell, and brought him back to Cairo. There he was hanged, shot, his body burnt, and his organs sold as souvenirs.

After reading accounts of this latest lynching, Ida, Ferdinand, and other black leaders gathered once more in Chicago. Ferdinand cited the state anti-lynching law, which had been passed in 1905. It required the governor to fire any sheriff who had failed to do everything in his power to protect a prisoner from a lynch mob. When the group reminded Governor Deneen of this law, he fired Sheriff Frank E. Davis. But Davis petitioned to get his job back. Soon a hearing would be held to see if he should be reinstated.

Ferdinand knew that two black eyewitnesses had seen Sheriff Davis signal the mob to pursue James, but they were unwilling to bear witness in front of the authorities. He feared a "whitewash" would allow Davis to regain his job.

After dinner one evening, Ferdinand asked Ida to travel to Cairo to investigate. "You may discover something that will prevent Davis from getting his job back," he explained.

"Oh no, not this time," Ida replied. "You know how they've been accusing me of jumping in ahead of men without giving them a chance. Well, I'm not about to jump in again."

Ferdinand looked at Ida calmly. "Well," he said, "if you don't want to go, that's all there is to it." Then he picked up his newspaper and began reading.

After a while, Ida went upstairs to put her youngest daughter, Alberta, to bed. Soon she fell asleep herself. But the next morning, her son Charles woke her early and told her it was time to get up so that she could take the train to Cairo.

"Mother, if you don't go, nobody else will," the boy told her.

Later that morning, Ferdinand and the four Barnett children waved good-bye to Ida as she boarded the train for Cairo.

That night, Ida stayed at the home of a black minister and his wife in Cairo. He greeted her warmly, but what he had to say about the James case shocked her.

"You know we don't think much of Frog James down here," he said. "We think he probably was guilty of the crime. So we're wondering why you came all the way from Chicago to investigate."

Hearing these words, Ida leapt to her feet. "Don't you know that to excuse the lynching of a man like James can only lead to more lynchings?"

Ida was so angry with the minister that she had him take her to the home of a more sympathetic friend. The next day, she found and interviewed 25 black citizens about the lynching. That evening, she called a meeting of Cairo's black community leaders. There she learned that a number of blacks actually wanted Davis to get his job back because his replacement had fired the black deputies who had been working with him.

Using all her powers of persuasion, Ida reminded the group of her history of leading the fight against lynching. Realizing that some feared the authorities, she convinced them that black Chicagoans stood behind them. Finally, she warned them that if they did not take a stand against the sheriff, they would be encouraging other mobs to take justice into their own hands.

Ida's words had the desired effect. She got the deputies who had worked under Sheriff Davis to sign a letter stating that Davis had failed to take necessary measures to protect the prisoner. She convinced others to withdraw their support of Davis. Now she had some evidence to present at the hearing.

Ida traveled to Springfield alone. Fortunately, a black attorney named A. M. Williams learned she was in town and offered to help her present her case. Together, they walked into a hearing room filled with white faces. On the opposing side were Davis, his high-powered lawyer, and a half dozen other powerful white men. Davis's petition to get his job back was backed up by letters and telegrams, newspaper editors, and a number of clubs. To Ida, it appeared as if the whole white population of Cairo supported Frank Davis. To make matters worse, a number of blacks had signed petitions supporting him, including one whom Davis's lawyer knew personally.

After Davis's lawyer presented his case, Ida made hers. She began by reading Ferdinand's legal brief, which restated the anti-lynching law. Then she followed with the results of her own investigation. She produced the letter signed by the deputies. It confirmed that Davis had not taken necessary measures to protect his prisoner. She also produced a letter from the well-known black man who had formerly supported Davis. In the letter, the man took back his earlier support. She ended her presentation by declaring that if Davis got his job back, the act would encourage more lynchings throughout the state.

When she was finished, Frank Davis himself shook her hand.

"I bear you no grudge for what you have done, Mrs. Barnett," he told her. Another man asked her if she was a lawyer. Finally, one man told her, "Whether you are a lawyer or not, you made the best speech of the day."

Several days later, Governor Deneen decided not to reinstate Davis. He had found that "neither the sheriff nor his deputies were disarmed by the mob," and yet they did not resist the mob.

It was a brilliant victory for Ida at a time when she badly needed one. She was celebrated as a "heroine of her age" by the black press. But she was not one to rest on her laurels. In the summer she traveled to the NACW convention in Louisville. There, she urged the women to endorse a newly created national organization, the National Association for the Advancement of Colored People. This organization, the NAACP, would play a leading role in the civil rights movement for years to come.

In August, Ida and her children went to Wisconsin for a much needed vacation.

CHAPTER 20

For most of her life, Ida had been committed to the cause of civil rights for blacks. But she also strongly believed that women should have the right to vote. In 1912, several pro-suffrage candidates were elected to the Illinois legislature. As a result, women increased their efforts to get a law passed which would grant them the right to vote in certain Illinois elections. This law was seen as a stepping-stone to national suffrage.

In January, 1913, Ida founded the first black women's suffrage club in Chicago, the Alpha Suffrage Club. In so doing, she had the help of two white suffragists—Virginia Brooks and Belle Squire. The focus of the new club was to encourage black women to help get women the vote. One of the ASC's first acts was to raise money for Ida to represent the club at a huge suffrage rally, which would soon take place in Washington, D.C. The highlight of the rally would be an enormous parade. There would be banners, costumes, and floats. Leading the parade would be a woman on a white horse.

Ida arrived in Washington as part of a large group from Illinois. The group was practicing marching when Grace Trout, the leader of the Illinois group, gave them some disturbing news.

"Our leader, Alice Stone, has advised us to keep our group entirely white," she said, looking straight at Ida. Then Trout went on to explain that many of the women did not like the idea of black women marching side by side with whites. It would be all right for black women to take part in the parade, but they must do so in a separate section.

"We would like to have Mrs. Barnett march with us," Grace Trout concluded, "but if the national association thinks otherwise, I believe we should go along with them."

While some agreed that Ida should not march with the rest of the Illinois women, Trout's remarks outraged others, including Virginia Brooks and Belle Squire. "We have come down here to march for equal rights," Brooks exclaimed, "so to exclude Mrs. Wells-Barnett on the basis of race would be undemocratic. If we don't stand by our principles, the parade will be a farce."

Finally, Ida spoke, her voice trembling with emotion. "If the Illinois women do not take a stand now in this great democratic parade, then the colored women are lost." She had been a member of Illinois suffrage organizations longer than many of the women there. Furthermore, she knew that many black women were suspicious of white suffragists. They feared that if women got the vote, it might hurt, not help, the cause of black rights.

Listening to these objections, Trout seemed to waver. Then she left the room to speak once more to Stone.

Belle Squire took Ida's hand. "Everything will be all right," she assured her.

When Trout came back into the room, however, she announced that Ida would have to march with the black delegation.

Ida was stone-faced. "When I was asked to come down here," she said, "I was asked to march with the other women of our state. I intend to do so or not take part in the parade at all."

At this, Virginia Brooks and Belle Squire volunteered to walk beside her as part of the black section. Ida appeared to agree. On the day of the parade, however, Brooks and Squire could not find her. Fearing that she had simply decided to stay away from the march altogether, they took their place with the Illinois women. When the women started to march, Ida appeared from the crowd on the sidewalk and assumed her place at the side of Squire. No one bothered her, and she finished the parade with the rest of the Illinois women.

Afterward, the Chicago Tribune carried a large photo of Squire, Brooks, and Ida Wells-Barnett standing together with broad suffrage sashes across their dresses. Each looked satisfied.

CHAPTER 21

A young man named Ebert A. Hall was looking forward to working in Washington, D.C. He had recently placed second in a civil service test for stenographers. As a result, the U.S. Patent Office had sent him a letter offering him a job. A long train ride took him from his home in Des Moines, Iowa to the nation's capital. However, when he got to Washington, he wasn't prepared for the cold reception he got.

When the director of the Patent Office saw that Ebert was black, he told him that there were no longer any openings for stenographers.

"But this letter offered me a job," Ebert protested and handed the man the letter.

The man glanced at it, then looked at Ebert. "Sorry, that letter was sent to you by mistake," he said. "The only openings we have now are for file clerks."

"But I'm qualified to be a stenographer."

The man looked at Ebert coldly. "I told you there are no openings for stenographers. The best I can offer you is a file clerk position."

Something about the man's manner told Ebert it would be useless to protest further. He knew that the only thing "mistaken" about the letter was that it had been sent to a black man.

Another man appeared. "Samuel, please show Mr. Hall here to Office 510."

Ebert followed the man into an elevator and then to an out-of-the way office on the top floor. There he was assigned the routine job of filing letters from patent seekers. It was a task almost anyone could have done.

Deeply discouraged, Ebert continued to work for several months. During that time, he was surprised to see separate washrooms and dining areas for blacks. When it became clear that he had no chance of ever becoming a government stenographer, he quit and returned to Iowa.

Sadly, Ebert's experience was common during the presidency of Woodrow Wilson. Born in Virginia, Wilson had been raised to think of the separation of the races as natural. When his postmaster, Albert G. Burleson, complained about racial tensions in the railway mail office, Wilson asked what he thought should be done. Burleson said that he thought it best to segregate white and black employees. Wilson went along with the idea.

As a result, federal departments began to segregate workers in offices, shops, rest rooms, and dining areas. Soon, the Wilson administration, to weed out black jobseekers, began demanding that all applicants submit photographs with their applications. To make matters worse, blacks suspected that civil service test scores were being changed. In Chicago, for instance, only 6 African Americans out of 260 passed the post office exam. This number was far lower than in previous years. Blacks felt betrayed, especially because they had given Wilson more votes in 1912 than they had given any other Democratic presidential candidate.

To protest this situation, Ida and another black leader, Monroe Trotter, appealed directly to the president. When they met with him on November 6, 1913, Trotter did most of the talking. He pointed out that African Americans had served in integrated federal offices for the past fifty years. He noted that segregation suggested that blacks were inferior to whites.

"We cannot believe that you would stain your honor or your place in history to satisfy a regional prejudice," he told the president.

Ida added only that they felt the need to bring the matter to Wilson's attention.

"I assure you," the president told his visitors, "the matter will be worked out."

However, the segregation in federal offices continued. Ida was disappointed but not really surprised. She and other black leaders knew that Wilson had personal ties to men like Thomas Dixon, author of The Clansman. This novel glorified the Ku Klux Klan. It painted Southern blacks during Reconstruction as brutal and corrupt. In 1915, it was turned into the movie *The Birth of a Nation*, probably the most racist film in American history. When Wilson viewed the film, he was heard to say, "It's all so terribly true."

Although Ida was disgusted by Wilson's racism, she wasn't about to give up the struggle. Back in Chicago, she turned her attentions to citywide elections. Now that Illinois women could vote in local elections, there was a real possibility of electing a black man to the city council. But first black women must be convinced that voting was worthwhile.

Surprisingly, some black men weren't all that eager to encourage black women to vote.

"Black women do not have to leave home to rule the nation," declared the *Chicago*

Defender. Black ministers, politicians, and other civil leaders also offered little support. But once again, Ida was determined. As the leader of the Alpha Suffrage Club, she set about teaching black women how the Chicago political system worked.

Standing in front of a chalkboard, she explained that the city was broken down into wards. These wards were further broken down into precincts. Precinct captains headed their own organizations, made up of a president, vice president, secretary, treasurer, and block workers. It was the block workers who were the "foot soldiers" of each ward. They were expected to know each area's voters and centers of influence, such as churches and fraternal lodges.

Ida knew that the most practical thing women had to learn was how to go door to door to encourage people to register to vote. This could be quite a challenge in some of the city's rougher neighborhoods.

"It's a terrible idea to ask our women to visit places where all types of illegal activity may be going on," the *Chicago Defender* insisted. But as it turned out, the women's greatest challenge wasn't the rough neighborhoods. It was the attitudes of men.

Ida was at club headquarters when teams of

discouraged women trooped in. "You wouldn't believe what some of those men told us," they said. They told Ida that the men had lectured them that they should be home taking care of babies. Other men accused them of trying to "take men's trousers." Some of the women were in tears at the hostility they faced.

But Ida knew how to win the men over. "Go back out there," she said, "and tell those men that you're asking them to register to vote so that they can help put a black man on the city council."

Why hadn't a black man been elected before? After all, blacks made up the majority in Chicago's Second Ward. The answer was that black men usually voted for white candidates, who offered them jobs and other favors once they were elected. This system was called "patronage." But black women seemed less willing to let white politicians influence them.

Still, there were problems. At the registration centers, women were asked to reveal their ages. Many had never done so before. But since the legal voting age was 21, some fibbed a little. When the wife of a well-known politician told officials that she was 27, a nearby reporter fell to the floor in a fit of laughter.

However, no one was laughing when the Alpha Suffrage Club got large numbers of blacks registered to vote. Seeing the growing power of black voters, the Chicago Republican organization decided to support a black candidate, Oscar De Priest. In the general election, De Priest was the only black candidate in a field of four. He became Chicago's first black alderman. Once again, Ida had helped to bring about real change.

CHAPTER 22

Every evening before dinner, Ida would skim through the newspapers. One evening in June, 1915, a story caught her eye. It was about a black man named Joe Campbell, who was being held in the state penitentiary at Joliet. Campbell had already been serving a sentence for killing a labor thug. However, his good behavior had earned him the status of personal servant to Odette Allen, the warden's wife. A few days before Mrs. Allen had been set to speak in favor of Campbell's parole, a fire broke out in the Allens' living quarters at Joliet, and she was burned to death. A later examination found that her skull had been fractured and alcohol spread on her bed.

The Allens' personal physician, Dr. Cleminson, was in prison for killing his wife. He also had access to the warden's living quarters. He claimed that Odette Allen had been raped and strangled—though he had not made a thorough investigation of her body. Largely because of the physician's evidence, Campbell was immediately arrested, handcuffed, put in a lightless cell, fed only bread and water, deprived of sleep, and repeatedly questioned. After forty hours, he confessed to the crime. Ida knew where his case was headed: death by hanging. Unable to eat her dinner, she went upstairs to think things over. As she was deciding what to do, the doorbell rang. It was two of her friends who were just returning from seeing *The Birth of a Nation*. Together the women expressed their outrage over the movie's unfair treatment of blacks.

"That's not on my mind right now," Ida told her friends. "What I'm worrying about is that colored man down in Joliet. I've just decided to see the editor of the *Record Herald*. I think he will help us."

The two women agreed to go with Ida to the newspaper office. When they got there, the editor, James Keeley, was sympathetic. "I agree it would have been strange for Campbell to murder the woman who was to plead for his release in a day or so," he told Ida and her friends.

After agreeing to print anything Ida chose to write on the case, Keeley took her into the city editor's room. There she sat down and wrote an appeal to the people of Illinois.

She urged them to withhold judgment until Campbell should have the chance to prove his guilt or innocence.

The next morning's edition came out with Ida's appeal in the middle of page 2. The first result of the appeal was that Governor Dunne had Campbell removed from the penitentiary and placed in the county jail of Joliet.

That Sunday, Ida traveled to Joliet to see Campbell. His face lit up when he saw her.

"You're the first black person who has come to see me," he said. He told Ida that he had been tortured into making a confession and that he had no lawyer nor any money to get one.

"Don't worry about that," Ida said, "We'll get you a lawyer."

A short while later, Ferdinand Barnett took the case. Every morning, he would leave home at 7 a.m. to get to Joliet by 9. He would arrive home by 7 or 8 at night. It was an exhausting schedule. After six weeks, Ferdinand took the case to the Illinois Supreme Court. He lost, but public pressure caused the governor to change Campbell's sentence from death to life imprisonment. Ida held out hope that he would eventually be freed. In the meantime, Dr. Cleminson, whose testimony had helped to convict him, was pardoned.

CHAPTER 23

"**S**trikebreaker!"

"Hooligan!"

These were some of the more printable words which flew through the air in East St. Louis in spring, 1917. The city on the Mississippi was simmering with tensions between white and black workers. White workers complained that the big meatpacking companies were bringing in African American strikebreakers from the South. Since the nation was now at war with Germany, some whites accused blacks of falling prey to "foreign influences." Blacks, of course, felt they had a right to earn a living.

In May, 1917, a labor union rally turned ugly. When it ended, an angry white mob poured out onto the streets and began beating any blacks who happened to be nearby. Two months later, four white men in a Ford drove through a middle-class black neighborhood, firing shots into houses and a church. When the car returned, blacks shot at it. Hearing word that a Negro riot was in progress, a police car sped to the scene. It was also a Ford. In the front seat were two white plainclothes detectives; in the back were two uniformed policemen. When the car appeared in the black neighborhood, it was fired on, and the two detectives were killed.

The next morning, an enraged white mob fanned out into the black community, killing, looting, and setting fires. Eyewitnesses saw whites shoot blacks who had earlier been beaten unconscious. The National Guard was called in but did nothing as children and men were killed and women stripped of their clothing. When the riot ended, nearly 150 blacks had been killed.

On July 3, 1917, the Negro Fellowship League called an emergency meeting. During the meeting, money was raised to send Ida to East St. Louis to investigate the riot and present the facts to the governor.

When Ida got off the train the next day in East St. Louis, she saw no blacks on the street until she reached City Hall. Parts of the city were still smoldering. At City Hall, she interviewed the head of the National Guard. He confirmed that the militia had been ordered not to shoot white men and women. Ida could guess that this applied even to whites who were attacking blacks.

As she was about to leave City Hall, a number of black women came into the waiting room. They looked dirty and tired. In talking to them, Ida learned that they had just returned from St. Louis. It was there, across the river, that thousands of blacks had taken refuge. Now the women were waiting for a military escort to take them back to what was left of their homes.

"May I go with you?" Ida asked the women.

They agreed that she could.

When they arrived, they found that many of their homes had been either burned or looted. Doors had been pulled off hinges and windows broken. What couldn't be carried away had been destroyed—pianos, furniture, and bedding.

The women gathered what remained of their clothing and loaded it onto the truck. When they were finished, the women asked the driver to take them across the bridge into St. Louis. He refused and instead took them back to City Hall. There, a Red Cross man listened to the women and demanded that the driver take the women to St. Louis. He asked Ida to go along to make sure that it was done.

Ida spent the entire day going with different groups of women to salvage what they could of their belongings and leave. That evening, she returned to City Hall, where a black janitor brought her a sandwich and a glass of milk. When Ida told him she was too tired to return to Chicago that night, he said there was no place in East St. Louis for her to stay—that all the blacks there were in hiding. The only thing that remained for Ida to do was to travel to St. Louis by streetcar. Luckily, she happened to run into some friends there and spent the night in their home.

The next day, Ida returned to Chicago and made her report to a crowded meeting at Bethel Church. That night, she and a group of concerned citizens went to Springfield. The following day, they met with Governor Lowden. Although he warned them against "fiery talk," he did promise to aid the victims and to punish the militiamen who had contributed to the violence.

A few days later, Ida again traveled to East St. Louis to gather more information about the National Guard's role in the riot. One witness described soldiers firing into a group of blacks standing near a restaurant, badly injuring one woman. Another victim told Ida that soldiers had driven him and his family out of their home. As they were leaving, he had asked how much money there was in it. It broke Ida's heart to hear stories such as these, but she knew that she must make as strong a case as she could.

As the official investigation got underway, Ida wrote up her investigation in a pamphlet which she entitled *The East St. Louis Massacre: The Greatest Outrage of the Century.* It opened with the stories of the four women she had first met and followed back to their homes. It included their eyewitness accounts of whites beating and killing blacks. All told, Ida interviewed around fifty people. She also quoted reports from white newspapers such as the *St. Louis Post-Dispatch.* This newspaper had reported vicious attacks by whites on blacks. She knew that reports such as these would serve to counter the argument that she was exaggerating attacks against blacks.

Despite national attention, however, it soon became clear that Illinois officials were going easy on white rioters and singling out blacks for harsh punishment. Eleven black men were each sentenced to fourteen years in prison for killing the white detectives. In contrast, four whites were found guilty of homicide, but received only five years in prison. Forty-one whites were found guilty of minor offenses and given short sentences or fines. A number of whites simply fled the area and received no punishment at all.

During the course of the trials, Ida realized that a black dentist named Le Roy Bundy was going to be made a scapegoat. When the white mob had attacked, he had escaped to Ohio. While there, he had been captured and returned to Illinois. Now, Ida and other black leaders suspected that, as the alleged leader of the conspiracy, he would be given either life imprisonment or the death penalty.

Ida urged the black community to help defend Bundy. "We must strike in our own defense," she declared.

Soon after her remarks appeared in the papers, Ida was told that Bundy wanted to see her. Traveling to Granite, Illinois, she visited him in the Belleville County Jail. He had been grimly pacing his cell, but brightened when he saw Ida. He wanted to know if she could find a first-rate lawyer to represent him. She agreed to do so.

When Ida returned to Chicago, she wrote an article for the *Defender* encouraging people to contribute to the Bundy defense. As a result, money began to pour in from all over the country. These funds were given to Mrs. Bundy, who hired an excellent lawyer to represent her husband.

This widespread national interest halted efforts to scapegoat Bundy. Thanks to the money raised by his supporters, he posted bail. This enabled him to travel throughout the country to raise more money for his lengthy defense. Although he was convicted in a lower court, his case eventually reached the Illinois Supreme Court. The justices there decided that his involvement in the riot was not proven. Bundy was freed. Not long afterward, he set up his dental practice in Cleveland, Ohio.

Although Ida had played a key role in winning his freedom, Bundy never thanked her for her help. Still, she knew that his release was a victory for all African Americans.

CHAPTER 24

On April 6, 1917, the United States entered World War I and sent troops to fight Germany. To some, this meant that all criticism of the U.S. government should stop. Not Ida. Although she aided the U.S. war effort by selling Liberty Bonds and preparing Christmas packages for the troops, she wasn't about to keep silent when she saw her people treated unjustly. This attitude would soon get her into trouble with the government.

Ida, like most black citizens, had a good deal of pride in the all-black Twenty-Fourth United States Infantry, Third Battalion. The infantrymen had shown their courage as far back as the Civil War. More recently, they had fought with Theodore Roosevelt in the Spanish-American War and served honorably in the Philippines.

When the U.S. entered World War I, the Twenty-Fourth had expected to be sent overseas to fight. Instead they had been sent to Camp Logan, near Houston, Texas. There they were given the lowly task of guarding government property. Also stationed at the camp were National Guardsmen from Illinois and the Eighth Infantry from West Texas. Members of the Twenty-Fourth knew that some of the Illinois guardsmen had attacked blacks during the East St. Louis riot. Racial tensions mounted when the black soldiers refused to go along with Texas's Jim Crow laws. Some refused to accept segregated seating on Houston's trolley cars. One black soldier was seen in front of a restaurant, tearing down a "Colored Only" sign.

On August 23, 1917, matters came to a boil. A black soldier happened to be walking down a street when he saw two white police officers dragging a black woman out of her house. A few minutes earlier, the police had burst into the woman's home in search of two black teenage crapshooters. The woman had objected to their entering her house, so the officers were trying to take her to the police station. When the black soldier protested the officers' treatment of the woman, they beat and arrested him.

Hearing of the incident, Corporal Charles Baltimore went to the police station to object. There he was shot at and then arrested. Somehow a rumor spread among the Twenty-Fourth that Baltimore had been killed. Then the infantrymen learned that a white mob was coming for them. Under the direction of Sergeant Vida Henry, about one hundred soldiers marched to the police headquarters, where a mob of one thousand whites was waiting. Henry ordered his men to fire. They did so, killing fifteen whites, including several police officers. Two black civilians were killed, as well as four of the black soldiers. Before he could be captured, Henry shot himself in the mouth, dying instantly.

This mutiny was punished severely. On December 11, 1917, thirteen of the black soldiers were hanged. In a second court-martial, eleven more were given a death sentence. Forty-seven were given life imprisonment.

Black leaders protested the harshness of the punishments. The NAACP's *Crisis* editor, W.E.B. DuBois. was especially outraged. He believed the men should have been given a chance to appeal their convictions. "Our government lets white murderers and rapists walk free while putting to death black soldiers," he wrote in a January, 1918 editorial.

When Ida learned of the executions, she tried to stage a protest rally, but could find no place to hold it. Finally, she traveled to Leavenworth, Kansas to interview the soldiers of the Twenty-Fourth who were imprisoned there.

When Ida spoke with the men, they told her that they hoped to get a new trial. In the article she wrote for the *Defender*, Ida eloquently supported their plea. She also expressed her respect for Vida Henry. "However wrong his actions," she wrote, "his bravery and daring will make his memory live forever in the hearts of those who know his story."

Later, when Ida returned to Chicago, she had buttons made that honored the men of the Twenty-Fourth. "I believe it's our duty to keep the memory of these men alive," she told one white reporter.

Soon afterward, there was another knock at Ida's door. When she opened it, two intelligence officers asked her if she was responsible for distributing the buttons.

"Yes," she replied.

"Then we must inform you that if you continue to do so, you will be arrested," the taller man declared.

"On what charge?" Ida demanded.

"Treason," the smaller man replied.

"I am not guilty of treason, but if you think I am, you know your duty."

The two officers were taken aback. Here was a middle-aged black woman practically inviting them to arrest her. In the end, they failed to convince her to stop distributing the buttons. And they did not arrest her. Ida would wear one of the buttons for the rest of her life

CHAPTER 25

One day in February, 1919, the Barnett family joined the crowds which lined Michigan Avenue in Chicago. As flags waved and confetti fell from tall buildings, Illinois' 370th Infantry marched proudly past. It was an all-black unit that had fought courageously on the battlefields of France and Belgium.

"Look, there's Ferdie!" Ida and Ferdinand's son Herman exclaimed. He had spotted the tall figure of his half-brother, Ferdinand, Jr., marching with the rest of the 370th. Although they called his name and cheered, they knew Ferdinand Jr. could not return their greeting without breaking formation. Still, they wanted him to know how proud they were of him and all the black troops. But how did the rest of America see the returning black veterans? The answer wasn't long in coming.

While the nation celebrated the end of

World War I, the number of lynchings in America rose from sixty in 1918 to seventy-five in 1919. Ten army veterans were among the victims. Several had been wearing their uniforms when they were lynched. But if white attitudes hadn't changed much, the attitudes of African Americans clearly had. More and more, black veterans were wondering why they were still deprived of basic rights at home. After all, hadn't they fought to make the world safe for democracy? Not surprisingly, many were angry and bitter. No longer would they be content to be second-class citizens.

Chicago's festive mood didn't last long after the postwar parade ended. As wartime industry slowed, many workers were laid off. Returning veterans, black migrants, and whites competed for jobs and housing. Since few new homes had been built during the war, whites were more determined than ever to prevent blacks from moving into their neighborhoods. Between January and June, 1919, there were fourteen bombings of black residents or realtors who sold property to them. But only two people had been arrested in connection with these violent acts. No one came to trial.

The rising tide of violence could be seen, too, in clashes between the police and blacks and between black and white industrial workers. In early July, Ida wrote an editorial for the *Chicago Tribune*. In it she pleaded for city leaders to act before the violence got worse. In her view, the root cause of the growing violence was injustice against blacks.

"I urge our leaders to set the wheels of justice in motion before it is too late; and Chicago is disgraced by some of the bloody outrages that have disgraced East St. Louis," she wrote.

Tragically, Ida's warning went unheeded. On a blazing hot Sunday in late July, 1919, a group of five black teenagers decided to swim in a section of Lake Michigan between the Twenty-fifth Street "black" beach and the Twenty-ninth Street "white" beach. When their homemade raft drifted toward the Twenty-ninth Street beach, a white man saw them and threw a rock. It hit one of the young men, who fell from the raft into the water. Although his companions did their best to save him, the young man drowned. When a white police officer refused to arrest the man who had thrown the rock, word of what had happened spread to the black community. A group of angry African Americans raced toward the Twenty-ninth Street beach and chased the white officer into a store. A white street gang came to his aid and began attacking the blacks.

By Tuesday afternoon, Chicago had erupted into a full-scale race riot. Whites launched violent attacks on black stockyard workers. Blacks pulled whites off trolley cars and beat them. When some whites tried to attack black middle-class homes, the homeowners shot at them. By the time the state militia was called, twenty-three black Chicagoans and fifteen whites had been killed.

What was surprising to some observers was that blacks had fought back. Ida, however, wasn't surprised. She knew that World War I had changed attitudes in the black community. As she wrote in the *Chicago Daily News*, the "Negro cannot understand why it was a brave thing to kill the Germans and not equally brave to kill white Huns in his own country, who take his life, destroy his home, and insult his manhood every step of the way in free America."

Although Ida hated violence, she supported the right of African Americans to defend themselves. In the long run, however, she believed that what would really put an end to racial violence was justice for blacks. This justice, she knew, would be long in coming. But she was prepared to keep on fighting. It was only a few months after the Chicago riots died down that she became involved in a new struggle, this time in Phillips County, Arkansas.

CHAPTER 26

In early October, 1919, white newspapers in the town of Elaine, Arkansas carried reports of a black conspiracy to kill whites. To put down the "conspiracy," members of the American Legion and other armed whites had attacked the blacks. When the violence ended, five whites and between 100 and 200 blacks had been killed. Afterward, 143 blacks were arrested. Others were told to go back to their jobs in the cotton fields and sawmills of eastern Arkansas.

A reporter named Walter White was the first to investigate the Elaine Riot for the NAACP's *Crisis*. White, who was very light-skinned, passed as white while he interviewed a number of white witnesses and officials, including the governor himself. But White's identity was discovered before he could interview the prisoners, and he barely escaped from Arkansas alive.

Still, White succeeded in revealing the truth about what happened in Elaine and why it had happened. For years, the white planters had been cheating black tenant farmers out of wages they had earned for picking cotton. The blacks had started a union and hired a leading white attorney to represent them. This had the white planters worried. Determined to put a stop to the efforts, they sent two armed white men to break up a union meeting. When the men attempted to force their way into the meeting, shots were fired, and one of them was killed. This event set off the white riot.

Although White's report caused widespread outrage, the Arkansas authorities convicted twelve black farmers of first-degree murder and sentenced them all to death. By November, it appeared that nothing would be done to save the men. At this point, Ida stepped in. She had the National Equal Rights League send resolutions about the case to the president, governor, and Illinois officials. She also spoke before a large meeting of another civil rights group, the People's Movement. During her speech, she read the resolution that had been sent to Governor Brough of Arkansas.

"Hundreds of Negroes have left Arkansas because of unjust treatment, and we pledge to use our influence to bring thousands away if those twelve men die in the electric chair," she read. She knew that Arkansas depended on black labor and that threats to get blacks to migrate north could be effective.

In mid-November, Governor Brough reacted to the pressure. He postponed the executions until a higher court could review the death sentences.

In December, Ida wrote an article in the *Defender*. In it, she called for the black community to unite to help the condemned men. She knew that the case might go all the way to the U.S. Supreme Court. Money would be needed to support the legal effort, and she called on her readers to contribute all they could.

"Let me hear from individuals, churches, secret societies, businessmen's leagues and women's clubs at once. Furnish me with the tools of war, and I will fight your battles just as I have done for the last twenty-five years." Only this time Ida was calling on blacks throughout the United States.

Her call worked. Since the *Defender* had a national circulation, donations began pouring in from all over the country. Somehow, the

December 13 issue made its way to one of the imprisoned men. Shortly thereafter, Ida received a letter from him.

"I thank God that thro you our Negroes are looking into this truble and thank the city of Chicago for what it did to start things," the letter read. Sometimes Ida felt exhausted by the constant struggle for black rights, but letters like this one spurred her on.

It wasn't long before she was headed to Arkansas to interview the prisoners and gather information about the riot. It would be her first trip south in almost thirty years.

CHAPTER 27

"Glory be, it's Mrs. Barnett!"

The black women who had met in a house in Little Rock, Arkansas were relieved to see Ida. They told her of their daily visits to the prison where their sons and husbands were being held. After hearing their stories, Ida put a scarf on her head and accompanied them to the prison. She knew the scarf was necessary because she wanted to blend in with the women—not reveal herself as the famous reporter that she was. The disguise worked perfectly. When the white prison guard looked up, all he saw was a group of unimportant-looking colored women who had been there many times before. He led them into the cellblock and went back to his post.

Once they were near the men's cells, the wife of one of the prisoners whispered to the men who it was who had come all the way from Chicago to see them. Their faces lit up with joy as they began to tell her their story. Still, by the end of Ida's time with them, the men were singing sad songs of death and heaven. It was only after she encouraged them to pray to live that they began to entertain hopes of freedom.

Ida spent two weeks in Arkansas. During that time, she gathered the information that she would later publish in booklet form as *The Arkansas Race Riot*. She also made it a point to meet with a leading black lawyer, Scipio Africanus Jones. Like Ida, Jones had been born a slave and had struggled to obtain an education. Since no law school in Arkansas was open to blacks, he had studied law under the direction of white attorneys. Now he had joined the defense team which had been organized by the NAACP.

Jones was very pleased to meet Ida. "You really got this whole movement going," he told her. "Before, I hadn't thought there was a chance of winning, but now colored people themselves are organized, and they are raising money all over the United States to help in the case."

When Ida returned to Chicago, she told readers of the *Chicago Defender* how much the accused men appreciated the support of the people of Chicago. Then she announced she would start a campaign to raise money to publish her pamphlet. When the pamphlet was published in May, 1920, it included personal narratives of the blacks who had suffered in the riot. One was the wife of Frank Moore, one of the condemned men. She described how she and her children had narrowly escaped the mob. Returning to her house, she found that the landlord had taken all her furniture and clothes. When she asked him to return her possessions and pay for the crop that her husband had picked, he threatened to kill her if she didn't leave. The wife of another union member was beaten and thrown in jail. A housekeeper who worked for a union member was killed and her body tossed onto a public road.

In addition to these chilling stories, Ida explained that the twelve men who faced the death penalty would have earned $86,050 if they had been paid the fair market value for the cotton they had picked. This sum would have been enough for the farmers to get out of debt and purchase their own land. The white planters had much to gain if the black farmers were out of the way. Finally, Ida revealed that the men had endured electric shocks and mock hangings to get them to confess or testify against others.

"This booklet goes into the greatest court in the world and before the bar of public opinion," Ida announced. In it she urged everyone to give the men a fair hearing.

Ida returned to Arkansas in September, 1920, to report further on the case. At this time, it was still going through the appeals process. From there, she traveled to Memphis, the city that had banished her thirty years ago.

CHAPTER 28

When Ida returned to Memphis in 1920, she found that the city had changed greatly in some ways but in others, it had stayed the same. Tall office buildings now set off the skyline. Automobiles cruised up and down streets where mules had once pulled trolleys. Electric signs were everywhere. Since the sale of alcohol had been outlawed statewide in 1909, saloons had been driven underground. Not surprisingly, the "bootlegging" of liquor led to more crime. By 1916, Memphis had the highest murder rate of any city in the nation. And, of course, segregation was now a fact of life.

Still, there were signs of progress. During the course of her visit, Ida learned that the NAACP had established a branch office in Memphis. Its leader was Robert Church, Jr., whose father had been a supporter of Ida thirty years earlier.

"It's an honor to meet you, Mrs. Barnett," Robert Church, Jr. told Ida. Then he went on to describe his successful drive to get more blacks registered to vote. He was particularly proud of getting more black women involved in his Lincoln League. Only a few months earlier, the 19th Amendment had passed, granting women the right to vote.

"Of course, the whites try all the tricks in the book to prevent us from voting, but we'll never give up," said Church.

If white Memphis was guilty of the same old racist tricks, Ida, too, had not changed; she was as outspoken as ever. During her stay in Memphis, she gave two speeches. One was before a large audience at the Metropolitan Baptist Church. The other was at Avery Chapel. Speaking at Avery stirred bittersweet memories for Ida. It had been here that she had once taught Sunday school with her murdered friend, Tommie Moss. Perhaps she felt his presence as she spoke. Whatever her sad feelings, she knew she couldn't dwell on them for long. She had always believed that the best way to honor the memory of Tommie and all lynching victims was to continue the fight for justice.

Back in Chicago, Ida continued her work with the Negro Fellowship League. One day a frightened young woman showed up at League headquarters. Ida had been giving instructions to the office manager when she noticed the woman.

"My name is Annabel Jones. Are you Mrs. Barnett?" the young woman asked.

"Yes, I am," Ida replied. "Would you like to speak to me in private?"

Annabel nodded as her eyes darted nervously about the room. When she was feeling more comfortable, she told Ida her story.

"I was born in the South twenty-three years ago," she said. "When I was ten years old, I was given to a white family. When the family moved to Chicago a few years ago, they brought me with them. For thirteen years, they have beaten me and forced me to work without pay. They have also forbidden me to go out on my own. I had to sneak out to visit you here."

"Thank God you did," Ida replied. "But how did you hear about the Fellowship League?"

"From a black man who does odd jobs around the house. He told me to ask for you if I made my way here."

When Annabel finished her story, Ida accompanied her to her employer's house. Although Annabel was still rather frightened, she took courage in Ida's strong presence.

Ida knocked on the door. A white woman opened it.

After introducing herself, Ida launched into her attack. "Are you aware," she said, "of how many statutes you've broken by keeping this young woman in virtual bondage?"

Before the woman could sputter out a reply, Ida demanded that she hand over Annabel's clothes and the wages due her.

In the end, Annabel's former employer paid her two years' worth of back wages. With the money, she found an apartment and a new job.

Despite triumphs such as this, it was difficult for Ida to keep the Negro Fellowship League going. The wealthy publisher Victor Lawson had been willing to help it get off the ground, but did not wish to continue his support year after year. In addition, a new black organization, the Urban League, had come to town. Now the Urban League had taken over employment services in Chicago's black neighborhoods. This meant that the Negro Fellowship League was deprived of a key source of income. Still, Ida feared that the Urban League was not interested in helping those who needed help the most. She knew that it believed in weeding out "undesirable" blacks. Based upon her experiences, Ida knew that people who were down and out could become productive citizens, given the proper support.

But the writing was on the wall. For a year, Ida had been unable to come up with the rent to keep the Negro Fellowship League afloat. And so, one week before Thanksgiving, 1920, she arrived at the Fellowship League only to find that the landlord had removed the office furniture, stove, and most of the equipment. The place she had put her heart and soul into for so many years was now an empty shell.

The closing of the Negro Fellowship League came as quite a shock to Ida. It may have also contributed to her poor health. A week after the Negro Fellowship League closed for good, she was taken to Provident Hospital suffering from gallstones. When complications arose, she did not fully recover for a year.

Ida was now 58, tired and depressed.

"All at once the realization came to me that I had nothing to show for all those years of toil and labor," she wrote in her autobiography. While bedridden, she reflected, too, on the loss of many dear friends. Her relationship with her children weighed on her mind, as well. Although she had done her best to be a good mother, neither her sons nor her daughters seemed likely to follow in her footsteps. Her oldest,

Charles, had little ambition and eventually became an auto mechanic and chauffeur. When her second son, Herman, graduated from law school, he briefly practiced law with his father. But Herman loved to hang around "big shots" and developed a gambling addiction, which got him into trouble with the law. Ida's third child, Ida, Jr., was a sweet girl but seemed content to work as her father's secretary. She never married or established a home of her own. The youngest child, Alberta, was very bright but rebellious. Although Ida wanted her to go to law school, Alberta had other ideas. She had seen the sacrifices her parents had made to the cause of civil rights: the long hours, endless conflicts, and numerous train rides to drum up support. She wanted nothing to do with public life. Instead she planned to marry, have children, and become a stay-at-home mother.

All this discouraged Ida. But when her health improved, she once again got involved. In 1921–1922, she became active in the movement to get an anti-lynching bill through Congress. The new Republican president, Warren G. Harding, had spoken out against lynching in his inaugural address. On January 26, 1922, the bill passed the House of Representatives. Despite vigorous campaigning, however, the bill stalled and died in the Senate. It was another bitter disappointment for the civil rights movement and Ida.

But a few years later, in 1926, Ida would play a key role in the success of an all-black union.

CHAPTER 29

As the white passenger got off the train, the black porter handed him his bags.

"Thank you, George. And here's a tip."

"Thank you, sir."

Although the Pullman porter's name was William, not George, he wasn't about to tell the white passenger that. It was Pullman Company policy that all black porters be addressed as George, no matter what their real name.

For years, the Chicago-based Pullman Company had been one of the nation's largest employers of blacks. George M. Pullman had started the company in 1862 as a manufacturer of deluxe railroad sleeping cars. These Pullman cars became famous when one was used to transport the body of Abraham Lincoln from Chicago to Springfield. With their carpeting, draperies, and plush furniture, they were soon seen as the height of luxury. To cater to his well-off customers, Pullman hired only blacks as porters. Many were newly freed slaves.

At first, being a Pullman car porter was considered a great job for a black man to have. The work was steady, and porters could boast of traveling around the country and hobnobbing with the rich and famous. But wages had failed to keep pace for Pullman porters. In the 1920s, they were earning $72.50 a month, while unskilled meatpackers were making $22 a week. Pullman conductors, who were almost always white, earned $150 a month. And, of course, being called "George," whatever your name was, was degrading.

Still, it wasn't easy to convince the porters that they needed a union. Some passengers gave generous tips. Employees had health insurance and a pension. But the Pullman Company could be mean-spirited as well as generous. Porters spent roughly 10 percent of their time in unpaid set-up and clean-up duties. They also had to pay for their food, lodging, and uniforms, which might consume half their wages. They were even charged whenever their passengers stole a towel or a water pitcher. Additionally, the company hired people to spy on efforts to organize the porters. Sometimes these spies attacked union organizers.

Since the Pullman Company was based in Chicago, union organizer A. Philip Randolph knew that obtaining the black community's support there was key to building the union. This support would not come easily, though, for several reasons.

In the first place, many of Chicago's black leaders were beholden to the Pullman Company. Over the years, the company had donated money to such black institutions as Quinn Chapel, Provident Hospital, and the Chicago Urban League. Additionally, since business was once again booming in the Windy City, racial tensions had eased. Black leaders feared supporting any movement which might again spark the "bad old days" of Ku Klux Klan meetings, bombings, and labor unrest.

Yet A. Philip Randolph, like Ida, understood the importance of fighting for justice. To him, Pullman's policies toward the porters smacked of modern-day slavery. Furthermore, he was familiar with Ida's long history of fighting for the rights of black people. And so, in September, 1926, Randolph sent her an invitation to the upcoming mass meeting of the Brotherhood of Sleeping Car Porters.

Ida was delighted to accept. To further lend her support, she invited Randolph to speak before her own women's group and publicly criticized the "narrow and selfish" views of black leaders who refused to support the BSCP. She was particularly critical of the publisher of the *Chicago Defender*, Robert Abbott. She suspected it was Abbott's ties to the Binga Bank which led him to deny press coverage to the BSCP.

A. Philip Randolph was grateful for Ida's support. He knew that she had built a powerful network within the black community, which could serve to counteract the lack of support among other black leaders.

The October 3 BSCP meeting was a huge success. During it, Randolph accused Abbott of betraying his race because of the financial connections between Pullman and the Binga Bank. The *Defender*'s circulation dipped when porters started to refuse to carry it on their routes. Abbott finally caved in and supported the BSCP, as did many of Chicago's other black male leaders. Porters who had once felt embarrassed or fearful about being in the Brotherhood now proudly announced the fact. Not surprisingly, union membership continued to rise.

By 1927, the Pullman Company had begun

to react to the pressure. It let customers know that porters were no longer to be addressed as "George." In a few years, the Brotherhood would win higher wages and improved working conditions for its members. Even more importantly, blacks from all different backgrounds stood united, for the first time, to fight for black rights. Their combined efforts to help the Brotherhood would serve as a model for the civil rights movement in years to come.

CHAPTER 30

In May, 1927, Chicago's black business leaders gathered to toast Ida and Ferdinand Barnett as Chicago's "first couple" of the civil rights movement. Sitting in the banquet room as guests of honor, Ida and Ferdinand were pleased by this show of appreciation. By this time, Ida was nearly 65, and Ferdinand was 75. Both were showing signs of aging, but neither intended to retire. Ferdinand was still practicing law, and Ida was still doing her best to fight injustice. In 1928, she would protest the stoning of a black Girl Scout troop at Jackson Park Beach. Later, she took action to keep a young black girl out of the Geneva School. This facility for female delinquents was known for its unfair treatment of blacks.

Nor was Ida afraid to try new things. In 1930, she ran for a state senate seat against two political veterans. As an independent candidate, she lacked the financial support of either Republicans or Democrats. As a result, she lost by a wide margin. Although the loss stung, she refused to become bitter. In her daybook, she wrote, "We may profit by lessons of the campaign."

Soon after her electoral defeat, Ida began another battle. This time the goal was to prevent North Carolina judge John J. Parker from being appointed to the United States Supreme Court. Not only was Judge Parker against the idea of blacks holding office; he also felt that blacks should not be permitted to vote! To rally against his nomination, Ida joined ranks with other black clubwomen.

"We will teach President Hoover a lesson," Ida vowed. Together she and the other clubwomen gathered 25,000 signatures on a petition opposing the nomination. The political pressure worked: Illinois senator Charles Deneen cast the deciding vote against Parker's nomination.

Meanwhile, Ida was struggling to complete the autobiography which she had begun in 1928. She worked on it every day, writing in longhand. Her daughter Alfreda, who was by now married, noticed the pages piling up on Ida's desk. One day, she asked her mother why she was working so hard.

"You know that current histories don't tell the truth about our people," Ida replied. However, there was another reason why Ida was writing. On a more personal level, she wanted to set the record straight. She was hurt that even black publications were failing to give her much credit for helping the civil rights cause. When the *Chicago Defender* published a list of fifty important leaders, Ida's name was not among them. Nor was she mentioned in the current edition of *Who's Who in Colored America*. She knew that her fiery personality had antagonized some people. Nonetheless, she had contributed greatly to the civil rights movement—and she wanted that truth to be told.

But time was running out for Ida. By early 1931, she knew she was dying. On Saturday, March 21, she returned from shopping earlier than expected.

"I'm not feeling well," Ida told her family and went to bed early.

The next day, Ida still felt ill and stayed in bed. On Monday morning, Ferdinand noticed that Ida's head was terribly hot and that she appeared dazed. When he called Alfreda, she immediately rushed to the apartment. They took Ida to the hospital, but she never regained consciousness. She passed away quietly in the early morning of Wednesday, March 25, 1931, at the age of only 68. The cause of death was kidney failure.

As large as it was, Metropolitan Community Church could not hold all the people who came to attend Ida's funeral. They spilled out of the church and along the pavement, waiting to pay their last respects in the chilly March wind. As Ida had wished, the service was straightforward and direct. The Metropolitan's minister, Joseph M. Evans, spoke of Ida's international battle to wipe out lynchings, and her tireless efforts to improve opportunities for her race. When the minister repeated, "She will be missed," the gathered mourners answered with nods of their heads: "She will be missed."

After Evans spoke, a representative from the Ida B. Wells Club spoke of Ida's pioneering efforts. She was followed by a member of the National Association of Colored Women, who praised Ida's anti-lynching work. Then a member of the Alpha Suffrage Club spoke of Ida's efforts to gain political power for blacks. At the end of the service, Ida's longtime friend, the well-known soprano Anita Patti Brown, sang, "Come Unto Me." The service closed as George G. Garner sang, "I've Done My Work."

Later, after Ida was buried and the crowds had gone away, Ida's daughter Alfreda gathered her mother's papers together. As she sat down at Ida's desk and leafed through her autobiography, Alfreda noticed that Ida had stopped writing in mid-sentence.

"How like Mother," Alfreda thought. "She worked until she could work no more."

Despite her earlier vow to be a stay-at-home mother, Alfreda did follow in Ida's footsteps. She became a social worker with a deep commitment to African American youth. She also played an active role in the Ida B. Wells Club. Perhaps most importantly, it was Alfreda who was responsible for finally getting her mother's autobiography published. In this way, she kept her mother's spirit alive for future generations, just as Ida had done for Jim and Lizzie Wells.